ELORA GORGE

*...the beautiful river has a never failing attraction,
and to those who love to study nature the rocks have a
wonderful story to tell.*

John Robert Connon, *Elora: The Early History of Elora
and Vicinity*

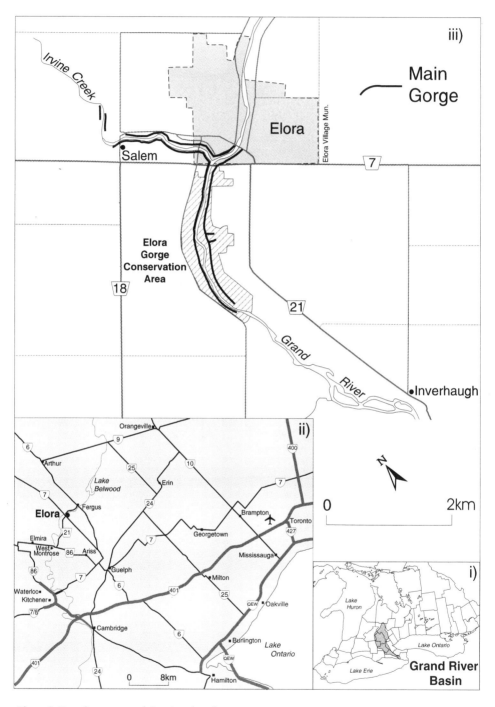

Figure 1. Location maps and "getting there":
i) Showing a general map of Southwestern Ontario
ii) Main highways and towns leading to Elora
iii) The main gorges of the Grand and Irvine.

ELORA GORGE

A VISITOR'S GUIDE

KENNETH HEWITT

A BOSTON MILLS PRESS BOOK

Canadian Cataloguing in Publication Data

Hewitt, Kenneth
    Elora Gorge : a visitor's guide

Includes bibliographical references.
ISBN 1-55046-123-0

1. Elora Gorge (Elora, Ont.) - Guidebooks.
2. Geology - Ontario - Elora - Guidebooks.
I. Title.

GB568.15.H45 1995   551.4'42   C95-931062-2

First published in 1995 by
Stoddart Publishing Co. Ltd.
34 Lesmill Road
Toronto, Canada
M3B 2T6
(416) 445-3333

A BOSTON MILLS PRESS BOOK
The Boston Mills Press
132 Main Street
Erin, Ontario
N0B 1T0

Photographs by the author
Maps and diagrams by Pam Schaus
Design by Mary Firth
Printed in Canada

The publisher gratefully acknowledges the support of the Canada Council, Ontario Ministry of
Culture and Communications, Ontario Arts Council and Ontario Publishing Centre in the
development of writing and publishing in Canada.

Stoddart Books are available for bulk purchase for sales promotions, premiums,
fundraising, and seminars. For details, contact:
Special Sales Department
Stoddart Publishing Co. Limited
34 Lesmill Road
Toronto, Canada M3B 2T6
Tel. 1-416-445-3333
Fax 1-416-445-5967

Front cover: Along Irvine Creek Gorge in fall.
Page 1: Along the Grand Gorge in winter.
Page 3: View over the waters of The Cove from The Cut, looking
towards Lover's Leap (Site 9).

CONTENTS

The falls, Islet Rock and Mill Inn at Elora.

R I V E R S C A P E

The falls at Elora separate two contrasting landscapes, one dominated by human history and the other by natural history. Above the falls, buildings crowd the riverbanks. They tell the story of some 170 years of European settlement, where water power, a convenient river crossing and scenic beauty have drawn people to this place.

Below the falls lies a totally different world, one of sheer rockwalls and swift water. The scene belongs to the river, a *riverscape* formed by the erosive power of water working against the variable resistance of limestone bedrock. Colour and mood follow the rhythms of sunlight, season and plant growth. Here, the story of Elora Gorge takes us back more than 400 million years.

This gorge on the main Grand River is joined, just below the falls, by another on its tributary, Irvine Creek. They are commonly referred to together as Elora Gorge. The two gorges, the deepest of the rockwalled sections of the Upper Grand, are among the few easily accessible and fairly unspoiled natural environments remaining in Southern Ontario. To reach them the visitor must pass along the ever-growing web of highways and urban subdivisions. These riverscapes are hemmed in by the rectangular scenery of fields and woodlots, and the quiet gardens of small towns. But in those final steps leading to the edge of the gorge, all that is left behind.

In a brief moment you travel through huge sweeps of geological time. Drastic changes in the environment of Southern Ontario are recorded in the rockwalls, fossils and caves. The riverscape is also a river of escape. It carries us into the remote past and opens a window on ancient worlds vastly different from today's.

Down in the gorges, the untamed ruggedness seems more remote from towns and cities than the actual distance suggests. Visible everywhere is evidence of tremen-

Along Irvine Creek Gorge in fall.

dous natural forces. The cataracts and rockslides tell you that not all are ancient. Flood and landslide may still suddenly transform the scene. But as you become accustomed to the gorges you can also seek out their hidden and sheltered places, where tranquil moments and many of the more delicate landforms can be enjoyed.

This book introduces you to the natural history of the gorges. It provides a portable walking guide with interpretations of selected features you will encounter. I have concentrated on the geology and ideas from geomorphology, the science of landscape. But this is not a textbook. It is written for visitors and local residents who want to know a little more about the gorges and the forces that shaped them. As far as possible I have tried to use everyday language and keep technicalities to a minimum. It is intended for anyone who takes pleasure in observing and inquiring about the landscape, and especially those who will simply enjoy exploring a unique and attractive riverscape.

The gorges are magical places. The more you look, the greater you sense a rich and fantastic story. But some of their magic is quite fragile, and if we are to share it with others and if it is to survive for future generations it must be treated with respect and care.

KEYS TO THE RIVERSCAPE

But how the Grand River and the Irvine, which here form a junction, ever cut such a deep course through so many miles of limestone rock is a mystery.

The Elora *Lightning Express*,
April 22, 1875

It was indeed a mystery back in 1875, but geological discoveries and the work of earth scientists in Southern Ontario have revealed much that lay hidden then. A walk in these gorges nowadays is still a journey of exploration. If you return, you keep stumbling upon undiscovered places: possibly a cave or rockslide behind a dense thicket, an animal trail, maybe a line of springs or, if you are lucky, a rich find of fossils. Come at a different season and all seems changed. Even so, the visible features of the gorges prove to be clues to their origin and history.

Behind the complex details of the riverscape lies a large-scale unity of development. The keys to that development may first be sketched out as answers to three main questions: What gives the gorges their distinctive appearance? Why do rock gorges exist here? What processes have created the gorges and continue to shape them?

The main Grand Gorge, looking downstream from The Cove.

ROCK CONTROL

The gorges owe their distinctive appearance above all to the local bedrock. This, the solid rock exposed at the surface throughout them, controls the typical features of river channel and rockwall. Bedrock largely determines where cave, cataract and rockslide occur. The rock itself is a type of limestone known as dolostone. While limestone is common in Southern Ontario, the variety around Elora is singular in its makeup. Why this is so takes us back about 410 million years and to conditions utterly different from what we find here today.

The Grand and Irvine gorges are cut through rocks that first developed on the floor of a warm, shallow tropical sea. The original constituents were largely remains of sea creatures. In fact, the rock is one huge accumulation of fossils. If many are no longer recognizable due to chemical alteration, enough good examples remain for us to reconstruct the life on the floor of that ancient sea. The singular features of the gorges record, especially, the presence of numerous organic reefs, forming resistant outcrops of rock along the channels and walls.

To imagine what this part of Ontario looked like when the bedrock formed, think of the Great Barrier Reef of Australia or perhaps the reef archipelagoes of Grand Bahama. Drowned by the sea, the region's environment in those far-distant times resembled today's great coral reef platforms and barriers. You will also find fossil remains of ancient corals in the gorges, but here they were not important reef builders. However, the long-extinct creatures that were, created forms that resemble present-day coral reefs.

The pale grey-and-white bluffs overhanging the Grand, which have long attracted painter and photographer, consist mostly of the larger reefs. Massive units of dolostone, erected so long ago by marine organisms, they give rise to features that single out these gorges from most others. In particular, it is the reefy dolostone that supports a unique development of overhanging cliffs with deeply eroded recesses at their base.

Rare in mountains, and rare even in other rock gorges, overhanging walls are the norm along the Elora Gorge. There are some 25 kilometres of overhanging cliffs leaning over the Grand and Irvine, or standing as old cliff lines and low bluffs some distance back from the present streams. All reflect the form and strength of rock masses that grew originally as colonies of organisms on a sea floor.

The gorges are cut through bedrock that formed as a system of reefs. For the most part, the strong, massive reefs resist erosion more effectively than the rock that formed in pools and lagoons between them. Many twists and turns of the channels record the river's struggle to find a path through the maze of reefs.

Because the rock is a limestone, it dissolves fairly easily in water, creating caves, holes and other solution forms. These tend to be located along lines of weakness or changes related to the pattern of reefs and lagoons, and to downcutting of the gorges through them.

When you walk through the gorge, and as your eyes adjust to the strange contours of its walls, you will start to read the story of the limestone directly. The cliffs are like an old tapestry, much laundered, its colours faded, but still depicting today a sea-floor world of long ago.

However, the bedrock itself was already more than 400 million years old when the gorges were first cut. It is hard to imagine a more drastic change in the natural environment than the one that brought this about.

GLACIAL FLOODS

How did the gorges come into existence? Conditions at the end of the last Ice Age seem to hold the answer. For many thousands of years all of Ontario had been under ice. However, roughly 15,000 years ago parts of the Upper Grand began to re-emerge from the shrinking ice cover. The Laurentide Ice Sheet actually reached and

Overhanging reef mass along the main Grand Gorge (between Sites 14 and 17).

crossed Southern Ontario as several distinct ice streams that also formed separate ice lobes at its margins. As the Ice Sheet melted back, one of the ice-free areas opened up between the lobes along the Upper Grand. In the short summers, great floods from the melting of the ice were routed southward through our area. Other drainage routes were still blocked by ice or by ridges of erosional debris deposited along the margins of the ice lobes.

Between Belwood and West Montrose, the water began cutting channels in the slightly more exposed bedrock surface. When the ice disappeared altogether, Upper Grand streams continued to flow toward and through some of the rock-cut channels, and have gone on deepening and extending them. Other chasms dried up or lost most of their flow when deprived of glacier waters. The abandoned gorges now join the living ones as dry relict canyons at higher levels. Rock gorges, perhaps from earlier glacial periods, now buried and filled up with sed-

iments, have been discovered nearby. One, found immediately to the east, is much larger than the present Grand Gorge.

EXTREME EVENTS: A FLOOD-CONTROLLED RIVERSCAPE

What are the processes that created and continue to shape these gorges? The gorges are primarily a result of the river's work in eroding and carrying away the bedrock, and of stresses on the rockwalls exposed by the river. Yet only powerful processes, capable of overcoming the stubborn resistance of bedrock, could create the channels and walls, and the direction the gorges have taken. If these processes are more successful where the rock is relatively weak, the sheer cliffs testify to the enduring strength of most of the rock. It seems, therefore, that extreme erosional events of the last 15,000 years have largely carved out the gorges.

The Grand River in flood. View from the left bank above the falls looking towards the Mill Inn.

Although found amid subdued terrain, the gorge landforms are like those of high mountains, principally cut in bedrock and littered with boulder-sized debris. As with the mountains, here, too, flood and storm, rockfall and rockslide play a major role. Only in these events are the high levels of energy reached that will dislodge or pluck rock from the walls and channels and sweep away the huge boulders. Less obvious, but equally important, large quantities of water entering fissures in the rock can critically weaken it, resulting in rockslides. Because of these circumstances, you could call the gorges extreme-event landforms.

Today, rock removal that is reshaping the channels occurs largely during high floods. In most years, the springtime snowmelt floods dominate the transport of boulders and finer sediment through the gorges. Concentrated floods of meltwater were probably responsible for the early cutting of the gorges at the end of the Ice Age. This is suggested by their unlikely path through the strong, reef-strewn bedrock and the existence of some large flood-excavated potholes high above the present channels. Meanwhile, visible evidence exists of the power of great floods in the recent past. Some of the largest boulders in Irvine Gorge have not moved since the greatest flood actually on record, that which followed torrential downpours of Hurricane Hazel in 1954. Others have not moved since the Grand River flood of May 1974.

Most rockfalls and rockslides also take place with the spring thaw and floods, but occasionally during snow, rain or windstorms at other seasons. Such events must have triggered many earlier and larger rockslides whose debris is still strewn along the floor of the gorges. Usually, however, the rockwalls and channels appear unyielding and hardly seem to change at all.

There are important yet less conspicuous features and removals of bedrock due to gentler and more frequent processes. The slow, continuous removal of dissolved rock

Rockwalls, rockfalls and bouldery channel, Irvine Creek Gorge between Elora and Salem.

- the dominant impact of extreme events, particularly floods and rockslides, in the continuing erosion of the gorges

In my own early, puzzled visits I did not guess at such explanations. Perhaps you had or will have the same experience. As you stroll through the gorges on a warm summer's day, noticing the mild trickle of water and admiring the lush growth of plants in many places down the river channel, it is hard to imagine the torrents that rampaged through in the spring, only a few weeks earlier. When you glance at the apparently timeless rockwalls, it is easy to assume that they record fierce events of a far-distant era. The old theory may, in fact, seem more credible—that some long-ago cataclysm, perhaps a great earthquake, created these chasms and the river then simply occupied them.

However, the gorges' story, as it now appears, is as remarkable as any fanciful catastrophe. Some of the events are unbelievably ancient. Yet the riverscape remains a living feature, changing perceptibly, sometimes dramatically, in our own lifetime.

A great challenge for visitors is always that first moment when they look down into the gorges. So unexpected are these deep chasms in the flatlands of Southern Ontario that they are bound to astonish and to suggest fantastic notions! And the surprise never quite goes away. Even those of us who live here feel it each time we look over the edge or descend into the canyons.

It is partly to do with proportions. The dimensions sound trivial compared to the Niagara Gorge, let alone the Grand Canyon. The principal Grand River gorge is about 4 kilometres long, the main Irvine gorge 2 kilometres. The gorges barely achieve a maximum depth of 30 metres; their width is rarely more than 35 metres. But when you stand there, staring down at the bottom of the gorges, or looking up at the looming cliffs from river level, the scale appears huge. The deep slot and the great overhanging walls dwarf the visitor, and suggest immensely powerful forces.

in surface and ground water may be imperceptible—except for the very hard water, which explains the purchase of water softeners by local residents. Yet solution of the limestone has formed many of the caves. Combined with other weathering action, it also helps weaken rock to the point where storm or flood can carry it away more easily. Nevertheless, it *is* those storms and floods that excavate the surface rock and so fashion most of the forms we see nowadays.

These, then, are three great themes to explore more thoroughly as you study the gorges for yourself:

- the nature of the bedrock and how it has controlled the development of the gorge landforms
- the legacy of the Ice Age, especially meltwater drainage from the waning glacier cover, that started the gorges

UNDERSTANDING LANDFORMS:

HOW THE ELORA GORGE CAME TO BE

Bedrock:
The Geological Setting

Bedrock is always an important part of the natural landscape. Often, however, covers of soil, weathered debris and alluvium mask its influence. In the Grand and Irvine gorges, bedrock is visible everywhere. The rivers flow in bedrock channels. The form and texture of the gorge walls draw attention to the stone itself. There is good rock here, hard and dry, with sheer faces for the eye to wander over. Slabs and bulging promontories of limestone hang far out above the floor of the gorges, indicating material of great strength.

THE GUELPH DOLOSTONE

The rock in which the gorges are cut, Guelph dolostone, is their most important land-forming material. The original constituents were almost wholly extracted from sea water by marine organisms. A large part consists of fossils in positions where they originally grew. The reefs referred to earlier are the most significant examples. Other layers and zones are derived from remains of free-swimming or floating creatures that settled to the bottom at death, or fossil fragments carried there by waves and currents—sediments, as we normally think of them. Some of the rock mass

also represents deposits of minerals precipitated directly from the lime-rich sea water.

Like most marine limestones, the original matter was changed chemically to the dolostone found today—essentially a replacement of original calcium by magnesium. This was the most drastic change in the bedrock's composition. Unfortunately for us, it spoiled many of the fossils. Also, countless small grains and even whole fossils were dissolved and not replaced. This left many cavities, or *vugs*. You will recognize different bedrock units by the presence of vugs of distinct shape, size and quantity.

Throughout the gorges, the rock has a highly uniform composition. Take a sample almost anywhere, and a chemical analysis will show nearly pure dolomite—generally over 99 percent. That helps explain the once extensive commercial use of this dolostone.

From one end of the gorges to the other, the rock represents a single geological time unit known as the *Guelph Formation*. It is roughly 410 million years old. The Guelph formed in the latter part of the Silurian Period, and belongs to the same group of rocks that form the prominent cliffs capping the Niagara Escarpment [FIG. 2]. The Guelph Formation underlies nearly all of the Ontario peninsula west of the escarpment. Most is buried beneath younger rocks, except for a strip 12 to 30 kilometres wide between the Niagara and Bruce peninsulas [FIG. 3]. But here,

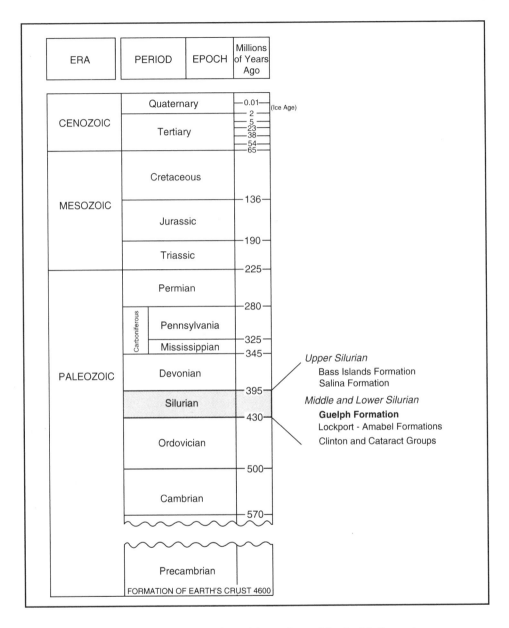

Figure 2. The geological column, showing the position and age of the Guelph Formation.

too, it is largely concealed under material deposited by glaciers and streams, or in swamps and old lake beds.

The Grand and Irvine gorges are among the most complete and accessible outcrops of the Guelph Formation. In all, they comprise some 40 to 50 metres vertically of the central beds, which is more than two-thirds of the entire formation. Almost continuous exposures occur over some 12 kilometres in a south-southwesterly line and for 6 kilometres in a north-northeasterly direction. Since the total thickness of the Guelph rarely reaches 100 metres, that tells you the

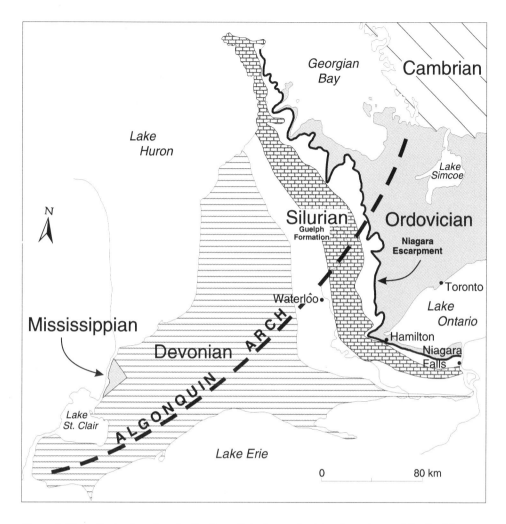

Figure 3. Map of bedrock geology for Southern Ontario, emphasizing the outcrops of the Guelph Formation.

strata are almost horizontal [FIG. 4]. A regional dip to the southwest is not obvious in the gorges, where local rock beds often dip in other directions.

A great puzzle about the special role of the Guelph Formation in the gorge landscapes is how the rock material is at once simple and complex. As mentioned, all rock outcrops belong to a single geological unit or episode. The composition is remarkably uniform. Moreover, the Guelph has been subject to very little of the kinds of earth movement that crumple and split bedrock and build mountains. Even so, the rock *is*

complex! Its intricacy is original, and derives from the growth and struggles of organisms inhabiting the Late Silurian seas.

REEF MAZE

A complicated pattern of reefs built a broad shallow-water platform at the margin of a much wider sea, which shelved gradually into deep water to the west of our area. Countless separate reefs, large and small, spread across the platform like a stony underwater forest. Between the reefs lay pools, lagoons and channels. They were like

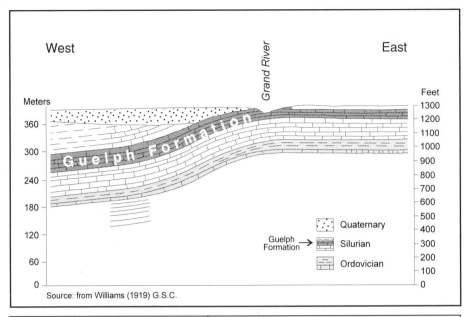

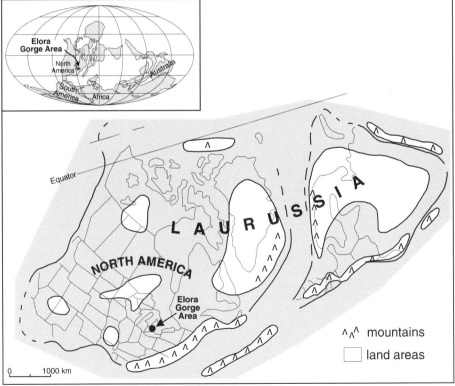

Figure 4. Vertical east to west cross-section of bedrock geology showing the Guelph Formation in the vicinity of the Grand Gorge (modified after M.Y. Williams, 1919).

Figure 5. Southern continents: a reconstruction of the position of Southern Ontario with surrounding lands and seas in the late Silurian Guelph time. Insert: World map of Late Silurian geography (modified after Geological Society of London, 1990).

openings in the stone forest—glades and thickets of smaller growths and deadfall of broken pieces of limestone. They offered pathways where the water might rush through at times of storm and small tidal changes. In pools and lagoons were great banks of shellfish and a myriad of smaller colonies of reef builders and other fixed organisms. Some grew across the sea floor to form tabular masses up to a couple of metres thick. Others gave rise to scraggy rock made up of innumerable modest colonies. However, most important of all were those colonies that coalesced into large, long-lived reefs, able to grow upward into the waves and resist their battering. These became compact tall reefs, the giants of this stone forest.

The Guelph time was ushered in by sea-level rise and the widespread drowning of the North American continent. These conditions favoured the expansion of reef builders and many other sea creatures. In the two million or so years that the gorge rocks represent, old reefs died off and new ones began. Reefs grew upon reefs, or flourished where only lagoons had existed before. The waves from sudden tropical storms occasionally attacked them, breaking off pieces of the reefs and carrying them, along with plumes of finer sediment, into pools and lagoons. At other times, pools were cut off from the main sea. Their increasingly salty water could be lethal to the reef builders.

Sea level fluctuated during the Guelph time. It defined the upper limit of reef growth. When the level rose, it allowed an upward surge. A stable sea, on the other hand, brought increasing congestion as reefs filled the available space. A declining sea would kill off the higher reefs. Evidently a net rise in sea level took place through the Guelph, allowing the build-up of the gorge rocks.

It is these conditions that explain why the resulting rock is so complex. You have to picture a complicated geography of reefs, and clusters of reefs, of many sizes, with irregular inter-reef areas. And the geographic pattern kept changing vertically from the older deeper levels to the younger upper levels. "Maze" seems the right word to describe this complicated three-dimensional puzzle, through which the gorges have excavated their courses.

Landscape History: The Five Ages of the Gorge

The landscape of the Upper Grand bears the imprint of several geological eras. Each was profoundly different from the others and from the present environment, which is busy putting its own stamp on the Grand and Irvine gorges. Five of these ages concern us. The first was when the rocks were formed. We have described the geological conditions, but you may well ask how they could have existed where we find the rocks today, far from any sea, let alone a warm tropical one.

ANCIENT GEOGRAPHY: THE GUELPH SEA AND A SOUTHERN CONTINENT

The waters where the gorge rocks formed may be called the Guelph Sea. But where was it located? Today's large, living reefs and most corals flourish in the tropical oceans. Sea surface temperatures must be high, normally between 25 and 30 degrees Celsius. That was probably so for the reef builders of the ancient Guelph time. However, it is not so much the world's climates that have changed in 400 million years as its geography and the location of Canada.

The Guelph Sea lay well within the tropics. Its latitude has been reconstructed at between 15 to 25 degrees *south* of the Equator. Along with most of what is now North America, it formed part of the southern continents [FIG. 5].

Nowadays these are latitudes of variable and uncertain winds, the zone known as the doldrums, and much feared aboard the old sailing ships. At noon the sun is high overhead throughout the year. Its rays are

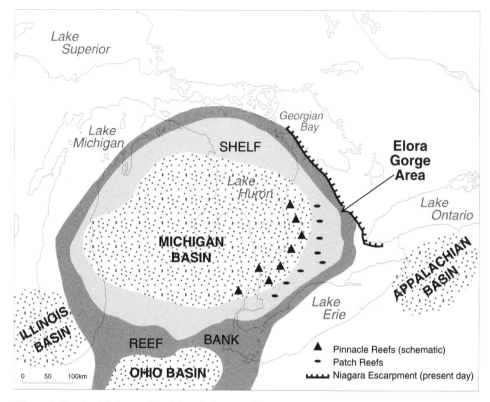

Figure 6. The Guelph Sea and reefs in relation to today's geography.

fierce on cloudless days. Calms and oppressive heat may last for weeks, to be broken by sudden storms that bring waterspouts and torrential rains. Tropical cyclones, or hurricanes, may achieve their greatest intensity here. The evidence points to similar conditions in the long ago Guelph Sea.

However, in those days the spin of the younger Earth was faster. A whole day lasted barely 20 hours, as a more dazzling sun followed a speedier course across the sky. The Guelph Sea covered most of what is now Southern Ontario. In the gorge area the sea stretched from horizon to horizon, but became relatively shallower here. At low tide, rocky cays and islets of porous white rock might emerge to be washed over by the waves. But no seagull left its telltale droppings. Birds were not yet part of the living world. In the blue depths of the water, looming outlines of reefs appeared and hints of the life that teemed about them.

The torrid climate was an essential factor in the development of reefs. So, too, was the configuration and depths of the Guelph Sea. Marine life is sensitive to changes in the water's depth, especially fixed organisms like the reef builders. The penetration of sunlight is critical, and limited even in clear seas. Reefs cannot form in the perpetual gloom at great depths. Hence, sea-floor topography helps control the places where reefs can form and flourish.

At that time, the region to our west, towards present-day Michigan, was sinking. Our own area sits astride an ancient ridge in the underlying rocks, the Algonquin Arch [FIG. 3]. This feature became more pronounced through the Late Silurian and helped decide the location of the reef platform and its rich development in the gorge area. The latter actually constitutes but a small part of a huge bank or barrier-reef system that ringed almost all of the subsiding Michigan Basin [FIG. 6]. It continued northward through the Bruce Peninsula, where you may see excellent exposures of the Guelph Formation and large reefs, and in a now-buried arc running down toward Sarnia and on into the United States.

Some geologists argue that this was not a true barrier reef because reef building continued into deeper water to the west, rather than forming a wall at the sea's margins. Farther out, on the deeper shelf, lay scattered *patch reefs*. Individually quite large, these did not coalesce into a continuous platform. Still farther out were reefs that kept pace with the deepening sea to form *pinnacle reefs* as much as 300 metres high and over one kilometre in diameter. Some of those reefs began life before the Guelph time and survived after it had ended. The patch and pinnacle reefs also became reservoirs for oil and natural gas derived from the ancient sea life. For many decades, the larger Guelph reefs were Canada's main domestic sources of these fuels—before being outdone by oil from even larger ancient reefs discovered beneath Alberta. Rumours of black gold in the rocks around Elora occasionally surface, but seem to be wishful thinking or a hoax!

To the southeast, the Guelph Sea passed into a deep trough, the Appalachian Basin. Land along its distant eastern flank included mountain ridges, mountainous islands and some active volcanoes. Their eroded sediment spread over the basin floor almost to the borders of Ontario. Much of the Guelph strata of New York state was formed in muddy seas and underwater deltas. But the sediment was excluded from our area, whose clear waters allowed a distinctive variety of Guelph life to flourish.

THE GREAT SILENCE: FROM TROPICS TO SNOW BELT

A gap of almost 400 million years separates the Silurian Period from our own geological period, the Quaternary. This comprises the longest episode and, in some ways, the hardest to grasp. Surrounding regions tell us something of what went on; how other seas drowned Southern Ontario, to be followed by periods of dry land. Rock hundreds of metres thick could have been deposited over our area and, later, eroded again. But no tangible record remains in the gorge landscape.

The most significant developments involved the whole of the Earth's crust. We have already seen the continent subsiding beneath wide seas and emerging again, in rhythms millions of years long. The other relentless source of change involves earth movements shifting whole continents and causing oceans to open and be consumed. That, at least, is the view of late twentieth-century tectonic theorists. They claim that the earth, its crust and its continents are highly mobile when viewed on geological time scales, implying changes of vast proportions in our part of the world. Since the Guelph time these processes have moved the region, at rates measured in millimetres per year, from the southern tropics to the northern mid-latitudes.

The world map when the gorge rocks formed, and the pattern of continents and oceans that existed then, was totally unlike today's map. Southern Ontario was about to become part of a huge continental area called Laurussia that included areas of Siberia, Greenland and Scandinavia [FIG. 5]. Most striking, at least to us, is the absence of an Atlantic Ocean.

Meanwhile, a supercontinent known as *Pangaea*, or All-Earth, was being assembled. Some 300 million years ago Asia, the Americas, Europe, Africa, Antarctica and Australasia were pushed together to form Pangaea. Barring small fragments of continents scattered over the vast ocean covering the rest of the planet, most of the land was packed on one side or hemisphere. In a sense, our own geological epoch begins with the break-up of Pangaea. That created the Atlantic Ocean and the continents as we now know them.

Through all these changes, the Upper Grand area was being pushed inexorably

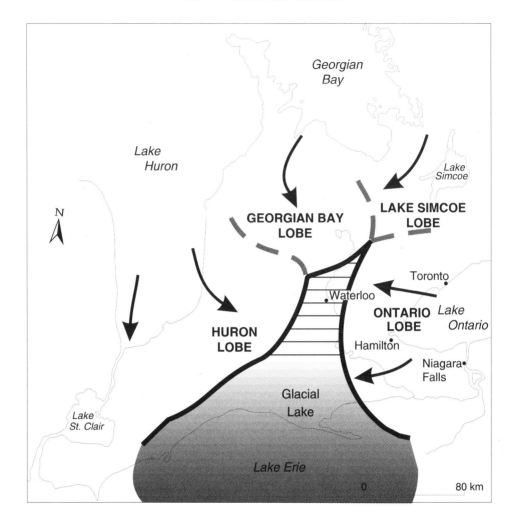

Figure 7. Reconstruction of Southern Ontario about 16,000 years ago, showing the various lobes of the Laurentide Ice Sheet and emerging Upper Grand basin (modified from Fulton, 1989).

into more northerly latitudes. Conditions were slowly put in place for the next major event, or third age, of the gorge area. Again, the environment was utterly unlike today's. But this time it *was* because of great changes in the world's climates, and the coming of the last Ice Age. And that did leave an enormous imprint on the landscapes of the Upper Grand.

END OF THE ICE AGE: BETWEEN THE ICE LOBES

Only 17,000 years ago, all of Ontario was buried deep beneath glacier ice. It lay in the grip of the Laurentide Ice Sheet. Flowing out from its highest regions between northern Manitoba and Labrador, the Laurentide ice covered nearly all of Canada east of the Rocky Mountains. Southern Ontario had probably been under the ice for 7,000 or 8,000 years during the last climax of this, the Wisconsinian glaciation. It was one of several major ice advances across the region, but it alone left clear and widespread landscape features.

The Laurentide ice passing over the gorge area flowed on far into Pennsylvania and Ohio, and was hundreds of metres thick at Fergus and Elora. Here lay an ice wilderness, snow covered for most of the year and showing no sign of the land beneath. The thousands of years of glacial erosion had excavated a rugged bedrock surface. Buried rock knolls and hills, revealed in well drillers' logs, probably represent resistant reef masses of the Guelph Formation. However, the behaviour of the Ice Sheet during its final phases, before retreating from our area, seems to hold the key to how the gorges came into existence.

Between 17,000 and 15,000 years ago, the Laurentide Ice Sheet melted back from most of the Lake Erie basin. In our area it began to divide into several great lobes of ice [FIG.7]. For many centuries, the Upper Grand basin lay under or between these lobes as they melted back and shunted forward unevenly. Early in this development, parts of the Upper Grand formed a narrow strip of land between the lobes, an *inter-lobate* area. A large part of the meltwater made its way southward through our area, since other routes were blocked by ice. We cannot be certain no earlier rock channels were here to help guide the waters, but it seems the gorges as we know them were initiated at that time. As the glacier waned, great floods of meltwater were produced in the slowly improving summers, to be channelled through the young gorges and to rapidly excavate them.

The full story is complex and unexplained aspects remain. At times, parts of the gorge area lay under the ice. Abandoned late glacial channels run across the present valleys. Other buried rock gorges were mentioned earlier. Dry gorges abound, as do valleys that seem too large for their present streams. However, the main lines of drainage appear to have been set before the ice left completely.

Following the disappearance of the ice, two related changes have helped control the development of the Upper Grand. In the earliest phase, after the ice receded, the river apparently turned westward just south of the gorges and drained to the Thames River. Later, the Upper Grand was captured by the Lower, taking it to its present outfall into Lake Erie. That created a significant increase in the river's average gradient. Although its mouth is only a metre or two lower than where the Thames reaches Lake St. Clair, the distance from the headwaters was shortened by some 150 kilometres.

The second development was an increase in the height of the north part of the Grand basin relative to the south. As the Laurentide Ice Sheet had built up, it caused the land to subside, roughly in proportion to ice thickness. With the ice removed, the land began to rise again or rebound in the same proportion, becoming more pronounced in a northeasterly direction. That means an increase of about one-seventh in the *height difference* between the Erie shore and the northernmost watershed of the Grand, or about 50 metres.

Thus, the basin has been getting steeper, giving more energy to the Grand and its tributaries. That may have been critical in the continued downcutting of the gorges. Any increase in overall steepness of the Grand basin is likely to have its greatest impact on erosion in the gorge sections. They not only comprise the steepest parts of the Grand River, but the rivers' ability to cut into the more resistant bedrock here helps to control erosion above and, to some extent, below the gorge sections.

THE PRIMEVAL FOREST

As the Laurentide Ice Sheet waned farther, the Upper Grand became part of a much larger ice-free area known as the Ontario Island. Comprising much of central southwest Ontario, it was an "island" ringed by ice on three flanks and lapped by the waves of cold glacial lakes to the south. This bleak and bare land was rimmed and crisscrossed by ridges of glacial deposits, marking temporary halts or small re-advances of the different ice lobes [FIG. 8].

Figure 8. "Ontario Island" with main glacier margin deposits (modified after Chapman and Putnam, 1984).

Once the ice left for good, the habitat steadily improved. Successively richer plant and animal communities entered and spread across the area. Some 10,000 years ago a forest dominated by fir and spruce, resembling today's more northerly boreal forest, had taken root. A thousand years later, that had been replaced by a mixed broadleaf and coniferous forest, with white pine, hemlock and oak. In time, maple and beech enriched the woodlands.

By 5,000 B.C. the major natural vegetation zones were close to those that persisted here to the early nineteenth century. The cool, snowy Upper Grand supported maple and hemlock forests, part of the vast timberlands that greeted the first European settlers.

Around the gorges lay trackless wilderness, broken only by trails kept clear by traders and hunters of the First Nations. This was the land encountered by Father Pierre Chaumont when he accompanied the famous Jesuit missionary and martyr Jean de Brébeuf through the region in the winter of 1640–41. Chaumont described slogging for days through apparently endless snow-filled forest, the way constantly hindered by fallen trees and frozen swamplands.

The Jesuits arrived near the end of this fourth age, during which the gorges existed but in a different state from the bleak post-glacial time or today. Round about grew trees of giant size, forming a heavy and largely old forest cover. That would greatly influence and, for several thousand years, slow down the pace of erosion in the Grand and Irvine gorges. Dense forest reduced flood flows, conserving moisture in the woods to sustain streams in dry periods. Above the gorges, the many undrained marshes and ponds, especially the once-common beaver dams, also impounded flood waters and smoothed out river flow. Fallen trees and log jams in the gorges themselves probably held back the flow and trapped much more sediment than we see today, except in the most severe and rare floods. Perhaps it was in this age that the main caves were able to develop. Many of them open some 2 to 5 metres above the present river level. They suggest that the river, the groundwater level and the flow of springs had remained fairly steady or were lowered slowly over several millennia.

Throughout this age the land was occupied by First Nations peoples, who hunted the beaver and burned and cleared parts of the forest. For a thousand years or so before Europeans arrived, indigenous farming people had grown crops and established villages on cleared land in the Grand basin. But their impact on the forests and flow of the Upper Grand was probably rather small, at least compared to what has happened since. Hence, though the region was by no means uninhabited wilderness, the Upper Grand perhaps warranted the description by some Europeans of primeval forest.

THE FIFTH AGE

Our own times make up a fifth age of Elora Gorge. It has involved some two centuries of drastic change in the surrounding landscape. The flow of the Grand River has been much altered and, if to a lesser extent, the Irvine too. Nearly all the forest cover was removed by logging, land clearance and fire. Early on, beaver were practically exterminated, their dams broken or left to rot. Agricultural settlement has involved hun-

In the primeval forest. Thomas Connon's painting of the Elora falls and Islet Rock as he imagined them before the land was cleared and Elora founded.
(Courtesy of Wellington County Museum and Archives)

dreds of kilometres of land drains, as well as ploughing the land and draining many wetland areas, all tending to increase and hasten runoff into the rivers. The drilling of hundreds of wells and the founding of towns and industries have all affected the rivers, a theme that will be taken up in a concluding section. However, in the gorges themselves the processes and conditions found today have, with greater or lesser force, controlled their development for the last several thousand years. The time has come to look at these landscape-forming processes.

Riverwork: Channels in Rock and Boulders

Natural landscapes are shaped by a wide variety of processes, many of which have played some role in the development of the gorges. However, the foremost have been

flowing water, especially the river and groundwater springs, and conditions on rockwalls. Let's concentrate on these two, beginning with the river.

This takes us to the changeable world of the riverbank. Here are some of the best places to see what is going on in the gorges today and to start appreciating elements of their geological past. The zone lying between the highest and lowest river flows is one of strong and decisive erosional activity and of sudden transitions. Within the space of a few metres the water may undercut the rock cliffs, froth around an accumulation of large boulders, slide into quiet pools or tumble over a cataract. You can see how the river's action has exposed structural details of the bedrock, and where rock is loosened by alternate wetting and drying. The main record of work by the all-important floods is seen in this zone.

Varied patches of plant life and a mosaic of contrasting habitats are encountered. Shoals of fish abound. In early summer, look for tadpoles. A little later, martins are found nesting under overhangs a few metres above the water. A blue heron stands motionless beside a fish-haunted pool, then flaps languidly away beneath the cliffs as you approach. A water rat swims past, intent upon its own business with the riverbank.

Movement and stillness seem more intense down here. Staring at the water as it rushes headlong over rocks or coils slowly

in deep pools is, by turns, exhilarating and restful. The scene captivates the eye, tempting us to daydream and drift in thought far from the busy world.

THE RIVER'S REGIME

The gorges mark the courses of the Grand River and Irvine Creek, and are a record of their work. They testify to the struggle between the power of the streams to erode and the ability of the bed and bank materials to resist erosion. The bedrock channels involve special erosional conditions and explain why floods, the most powerful events along the river, have such an important role.

The power of any river depends firstly on the flow of water passing along it. The flow, in turn, depends on the climate and the size of the basin. The Grand, which drains some 6,800 square kilometres, is the largest river basin in southwestern Ontario [FIG. 9]. About one-sixth—nearly 1,200 square kilometres—lies above the gorges and drains into them. Much of the upper basin has a gentle topography, but it is both the higher and wetter part. It supplies more than one-sixth of the Grand's flow.

Climate determines water supply over the year and the river's regime, or typical pattern of flows. Moreover, detailed records dating back some decades show that the Grand has a flood-prone regime [FIG. 10]. A large fraction of all the water that runs off does so in floods, especially in springtime. Then, the melting of winter snow usually results in at least one large flood in every year. It tends to coincide with the break-up of river ice. When this happens, the flow can be interrupted by broken slabs of ice wedged into narrows or against bridges and weirs. Often the ice jams burst suddenly and water backed up behind them rushes downstream as a steep wave of exceptional erosive power.

Spring rainstorms, when the basin is still soaked from snowmelt, can cause unusually strong floods. Such conditions gave rise to the most recent major flood—

the second largest on record—in May 1974 [FIG. 11]. Sections of river channel were shifted from one side of the gorge to the other, and some of the larger boulders moved, if only a few metres.

Summer thunderstorms may produce flash floods. Probably the greatest floods since the glaciers disappeared have derived from massive storms originating as Atlantic hurricanes that survive into the continental interior. These occur in summer and early fall. The largest rainfall and flood flows on record for Southern Ontario and the Grand River came during Hurricane Hazel on the night of October 15–16, 1954. As much as 23 centimetres of rain fell in the upper basin in 24 hours. People living on the edge of Irvine Creek swear that they have never heard such a roar as came from the river that night. Damage and changes wrought by the flood are still visible today. They include the tumbled concrete piers of a destroyed footbridge that once linked downtown Elora to the Arena, some high banks of now overgrown boulders and evidence of the largest boulders in the channels being moved.

RIVERS IN ROCK

The gorges are no more flood prone than the Grand's streams above or below. However, the river's power is also affected by channel gradient and channel form. The average gradient of the Grand from source to mouth is a bit more than one metre per kilometre. But the gorge sections are much steeper, nearly 5 metres per kilometre. Much of the actual descent is even steeper, occurring at cataracts and rapids. As flood waters rage over the falls at Elora and race through the rapids farther down, this adds greatly to their erosive power. The narrow rock canyons act like a rigid conduit for the water. No flood plain exists down in the gorges to let the water spread out. The deeper the water, the more concentrated its energy and the swifter its flow.

In that way a sort of balance is struck. Until stream power reaches a fairly high

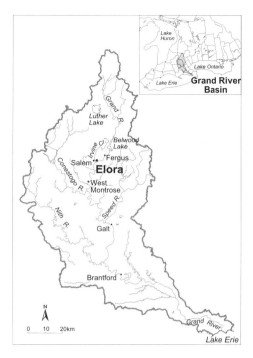

Figure 9. Map of Grand River Basin.

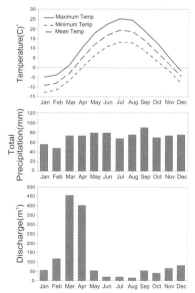

Figure 10. *Annual variation in maximum and minimum temperatures, and average monthly precipitation at the Elora Research Station, and average monthly flows for Irvine Creek at Salem.* (Data courtesy of the Grand River Conservation Authority and Elora Research Station)

level, it cannot overcome the resistance of the bedrock, nor move the heavy boulders in the channel. But the steep, narrow channels provide the river with greater power. In flood, the water acquires the energy it needs to erode bedrock and move large boulders.

Flood waters at Middle Cataract (Site 14).

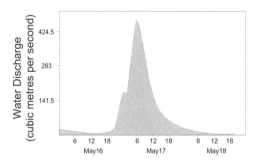

Figure 11. Graph of river flows in Irvine Creek during the May 1974 flood. (Data courtesy of the Grand River Conservation Authority)

Of course, the river goes on working at other times through less vigorous but more frequent processes. Repeated wetting and drying between low and high flow levels, along with freezing and thawing of moisture in winter, weaken the rock and make it more vulnerable in flood and storm. In the permanently wet channel limestone is almost always being dissolved or picked at by algae.

Nevertheless, it is the floods which do the main job of removing the rock and transporting or reworking the bouldery sediment. Boulders and bedrock can be loosened and plucked out by forces set up by fast flowing water itself. However, debris whipped along in the current does most of the erosional work. Boulders rolling and bumping over the bed can deliver hammer blows upon protruding knolls of rock. Sand and silt, swept along like a blizzard of fine particles in the turbulent flow, scratch and polish the rock bed. These, and concentrated dissolving of rock in areas of fast flow, create the streamlined forms you can see in the channels at low water. Along the gorges lie many large and small circular depressions or *potholes*. Debris trapped in the holes is whirled around by the current, especially in floods, and, in effect, drills the holes deeper.

On the gorge floors, after the spring runoff or following floods, you can see multiple patches of fresh rock where pieces have been pulled or knocked out. Only a small fraction of the whole channel area may be affected. But when projected onto a geological time scale, it represents a rapid rate of erosion, sufficient to account for 2 to 5 metres of downcutting since the Ice Sheet left. The rate varies with the resistance of the rock bed and its slope. Meanwhile, I think erosion rates are higher today than in much of the heavily forested, pre-European age, or, rather, are higher on the Irvine and were so on the Grand at least until the Shand Dam was built.

BOULDERS IN THE STREAM

Nearly all of the load of mud and sand carried from the country above the gorges is flushed right through them. However, patches or bars of bouldery material occur at bends and constrictions, or where the gradient is suddenly reduced. These bars, too, are characteristic landforms of the gorges.

If you examine them carefully, you will see that these deposits are not just random

Clockwise from left: rock bed stream, the lower Irvine Creek Gorge; spring flood waters at the falls, Elora; the main Grand Gorge, opposite and upstream of High Lookout (Site 11).

jumbles of boulders. They are organized. Groups of boulders are lined up or stacked against one another. Often a large boulder serves as a keystone against which the remainder are jammed. They may be piled one behind the other in an upstream direction. The boulders may be wedged, corner against corner, across the stream. Sometimes a major flood will leave "ribs" of boulders from bank to bank. At first you think someone placed them there as stepping stones or little weirs. But some of the boulders are much too large to have been lifted by a person. This natural stacking of stone against stone shows they were jammed into position by the force of the stream alone, and at times of flood.

CATARACTS AND WHITE WATER

Another notable feature of the rock bed channels is their sudden steepening into cataracts and their change from smooth flow to turbulent white water. The main Grand and Irvine form no true waterfalls, no free-falling streams. The water always remains in contact with the rock, rushing over a gradually steepening convex rock lip—including the "falls" at Elora! Nevertheless, in flood these sudden descents become ferocious. Even at low flows, the water tumbles and froths over the steep rock and churns in plunge pools at its base.

The cataracts reflect two important aspects of the development of the gorge landscape. Most cataracts drop over the edge of reef masses. These are places where gorge cutting is delayed by more resistant rock. However, the cataracts also represent phases in upstream migration of gorge deepening. This happens comparatively quickly in weak rock and is checked at the more massive reefs. You can readily see how the falls at Elora have retreated through the bedrock, extending the deeper gorge below.

Overhanging rockwalls along the Grand, downstream from the base of the falls, Elora.

Rockwalls: The Strong and the Weak

If the river made the Grand gorges, steep rockwalls are their most striking landforms. The cliffs create the prevailing mood in the gorges. Sheer walls rise from the river, starkly white beneath a dark fringe of cedars. Each shift in the sun's angle, each passing cloud, bring sudden changes in the cliffs' appearance. Early and late in the day the water is cloaked in their deep shadows. The rockwalls frame a unique landscape. Meanwhile, their significance for its development is out of all proportion to their share of land area.

ROCK-CONTROLLED LANDFORMS

The gorge walls exist because of the power of erosion. They record past onslaughts by the river, its abrading, dissolving, quarrying and removal of rock. And yet, such cliffs testify to the strength of the rock. Their form and height depict how well the dolostone has withstood the forces that combine to throw it down. In this way, the rockwall speaks directly of the main struggle that holds the natural landscape in its grip.

The cliff is a natural form of strong architecture, standing in walls comparable to those of great fortresses and cathedrals. Landform science emphasises this by calling the rockwall a *strength equilibrium slope*. The equilibrium, or ability to remain stable over extended periods, occurs at a steepness which other parts of the landscape will not support.

THE CLIFFS AND THE RIVER

The Grand streams brought the rockwalls of the gorges into existence. If first we consider a rockwall in its relation to the river, it may be called *active*, *inactive* or *relict*.

Active walls are found where the river now washes their base. Whenever it has

The Stone Sidewalk, showing the overhanging relict cliff and natural pathway below (Site 23).

the power, the water can immediately erode the rock and carry away debris that falls from above. To come into existence at all, cliffs must be active at some time. However, the stream channel may shift and abandon one side of the gorge. The rockwall there becomes inactive. Weathered debris and rockfalls may pile up undisturbed at the base, sometimes for decades or even centuries. In time a steep ramp of weathered and fallen debris called *talus* may develop. Terraces or gravel bars of river-borne debris may accumulate below the inactive cliff too. Vegetation finds it easier to colonize this part of the gorge floor. Later, though, the river may shift back to reactivate this side, rapidly removing the amassed debris and again attacking the rockwall.

Evidence of shifts from active to inactive exists all along the gorges. Most shifts result from floods and large rockfalls, another example of the importance of extreme events. Where larger rockslides spill down into the river, they tend to direct its flow toward the opposite bank and protect the slope from which they fell. They act much like artificial walls used in erosion control, the groynes and gabions you may see constructed along river banks and beaches to protect them.

Over the centuries, or where the river cuts down very quickly, an inactive cliff may be abandoned altogether. The river becomes so incised along one side of the gorge that even if it is forced back toward the other, it does not reach the base of the inactive cliff. Such an abandoned cliff has now become relict. You can see extensive sections of relict cliff above the present gorges, especially on the left bank of the Grand for several kilometres below the falls at Elora. In places they create the peculiar natural stone sidewalks described in Walk III. The relict cliffs record higher, more ancient, locations of the rivers. They suggest that much of the main Grand Gorge has been migrating toward the right or west flank for many millennia.

POTTERS' ROCKS AND CORNICES

The profiles of overhanging cliff create a set of landforms special to the gorges. Nor is it an accident that some recall the well-known Flowerpot Island on the Bruce Peninsula. There the "flowerpot" involves overhanging rock of similar origin and from the same geological formation as in the gorges.

There is a huge variety of rounded, bulging rock shapes that overhang the gorges and that resemble the profiles of urns, jars, vases, jugs and other pottery vessels [FIG. 12]. The analogy of form is not to imply that ancient potters, nor the fine ones in Elora today, copied these natural forms. But it helps prepare your eye to identify and sort out the range of otherwise unfamiliar cliff shapes.

What the forms record is one of our major themes—rock control. The overhangs depend upon the character of the bedrock and its relative resistance to collapse. The

A rockfall that occurred along Irvine Creek in the spring of 1985, near David Street Bridge (Site 5).

rounded, pot-like shapes reflect the strength and forms of the more massive reefs.

Rectangular overhangs or cornice-like forms are common in some areas too. There are places where overhanging slabs form almost continuous cornices for half a kilometre or more. They protrude to such a remarkable extent you can walk under them out of the rain. In some cases the vase-like and cornice overhangs combine.

UP THE WALL:
STRESS AND PARTINGS

The forms and steepness of the rockwalls do not vary much among active, inactive or relict examples. The strong bedrock gives the cliffs some permanence; they have lives of their own, resisting or responding to slope processes rather than the river.

The many kilometres of steep, often overhanging, walls indicate rock of unusual strength. The dolostone itself is quite strong. However, resistance to erosion depends even more on divisions or *partings* in the rock. They tend to be planes of weakness where the rock is most likely to break apart. Partings open up as erosion uncovers the rock. Water seeps through them; ice may form in them; tree roots force a way along them. For rock to stand in steep walls, it must have either few partings or none, or the partings must be arranged so as not to promote collapse.

Most limestones have *bedding planes*, partings that originate between more or less horizontal layers of sediment or organic growth. They are the principal source of weakness. Since layered rocks may be tilted and folded before exposure in the landscape, bedding planes can dip at every conceivable angle [FIG. 13]. Cliffs are subject to easier collapse if the planes dip toward their face. Planes that dip gently into the cliffs create stable walls, and so do the flat-lying beds which predominate in the gorges.

The other important partings are called *joints*. They may have formed at the time of compaction, when the original material changed into rock, or from pressures deep in the earth, or due to stress release as erosion uncovers the rock. The intersection of bedding and joint planes defines the size of

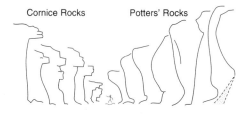

Figure 12. Potters' and cornice rocks: some typical vertical profiles of cliffs in Elora Gorge.

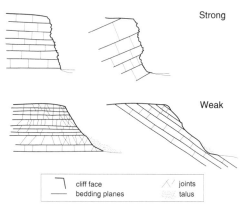

Figure 13. Relations between the dip of layered rocks and the stability of cliff faces.

rock units most readily exploited by weathering. The geometry and textures of the cliffs often reflect the density of partings in the rock. The flat-lying beds with more or less vertical joints that occur in the gorges form fairly stable cliffs. The complicated mix of massive and thin units in the Guelph dolostone also encourages the formation of steps and overhangs.

However, it is the main reefs, with few or no partings, that make for exceptionally strong walls able to support huge overhangs.

THE SELF-PROPAGATING GORGE

A distinctive system of fractures actually arises from the erosion of the gorge itself. As a gorge is excavated, the reduced confining pressure on rock exposed on the walls results in *stress release fractures*. Vertical or nearly so, they run roughly parallel to the gorge walls. Some of the best places to see the fractures are in caves. Once you are inside, you will notice that a main cave often opens out into one or several narrow secondary caves to right or left, or even overhead. There may be more than one set of fractures, usually found between 1 metre and 10 metres back from the cliff face.

The river excavated the original canyon. But release fractures become the main surfaces along which the large rockfalls and slides break away. In many places, the walls from which they descend are remarkably straight and smooth, disclosing the inner face or plane of a pressure release fracture. These fractures came into existence with the creation of the gorge. Thereafter, they propagate its shape and are a major factor in the retreat of the gorge walls.

ROCKFALLS AND ROCKSLIDES

The gorges are rockfall country, as surely as any high mountain valley. Below the gorge walls the debris of countless rockfalls has left ramps of boulders. At intervals you see huge broken slabs from past slides.

The scale and form of a rockfall or slide tell you something about its bedrock source. Larger slides arise mostly in the more massive reef limestone and thick tabular beds. Ramps of smaller, rubble-like debris tend to occur beneath outcrops of the less massive inter-reef rock.

Rock may start to move by simply dropping from a vertical or overhanging cliff. If the cliff is inactive, with a low-angle apron below, the rockfall may bounce on down or turn into a rockslide. In typical large rockslides, the beds become tilted back and spread out laterally down the apron, the outermost pieces spilling into the river [FIG. 14].

In many places tree roots seem to have pried the rock apart and may be critical in weakening it. Where trees lean over the gorges, rockfalls sometimes occur with high

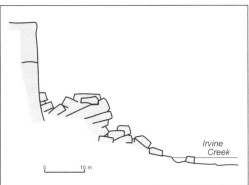

Irvine
Creek

0 _____ 10 m

Figure 14.

winds or heavy snow loads that sweep trees over the cliff, carrying pieces of rock among torn-up roots.

Most of the larger rockfalls whose rubble lies on the gorge floors are hundreds of years old—maybe thousands in some cases. However, countless small rockfalls take place each year. And in the past 15 years, I

have recorded five falls of over 50 cubic metres. We lack the evidence to say if these events are happening more often now than in the past, or less. What we do know is that the work continues.

CAVES AND OTHER KARST FORMS

Caves and other features formed by the dissolving of limestone bedrock are usually called *karst*. Compared to other parts of the world, the Grand gorges contain only very modest contributions to karst landscapes. Yet the dissolving of the rock has left many small and medium-sized caves and other distinctive features to explore. Some caves harbour small dripstone formations of stalactite (growing downward) and stalagmite (growing upward).

Perhaps the more extensive and distinctive of visible features result not from the dissolving, but from the deposition of lime from groundwater. Aprons of limy material deposited by springs are found in the mouths of many caves and where springs emerge beneath overhanging rock. There are places along the Grand Gorge with almost continuous aprons for hundreds of metres. But you have to search for them. Most are hidden in recesses beneath large overhangs. This material is called travertine, calcium carbonate precipitated from the spring water. It only forms where the springs flow all year round. Algae and mosses grow wherever this occurs. And if they depend on the aprons for their existence, they are in turn essential in forming them. If springs dry up or the plants die off, the soft travertine becomes rock hard.

These are vitally important parts of the ecology of the gorge area, supporting distinctive plant communities. Where it is being actively formed, the travertine is soft and porous. A remarkable fact is that throughout the winter plant growth on the aprons continues, kept warm and watered by the springs. The algae and mosses remain green, even beneath a cover of ice.

Opposite page, top: Rotational rockslide, lower Irvine Creek Gorge (Site 7). Below, Figure 14: Schematic long-profile of rotational rockslide, lower Irvine Creek Gorge (Site 7). This page, top: Travertine aprons developed along the spring line beneath a massive undercut reef, main Grand Gorge (near Site 17). Below: Overhanging and deeply recessed walls of The Cove, Main Grand Gorge (Site 9).

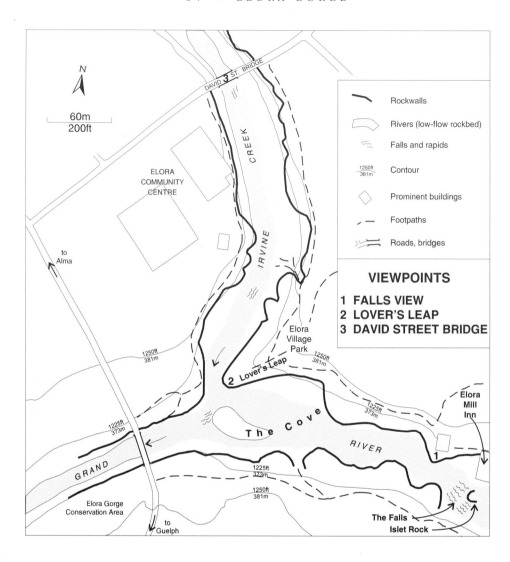

Figure 15. A map of the gorges at Elora village and the three classic viewpoints.

THE ELORA GORGE:
SEEING IT FOR YOURSELF

The best way to learn more about the Grand gorges is to visit them yourself. This book introduces you to some of their features and history, but there is no substitute for first-hand observation.

A road map [FIG. 1, p. 2] will help in reaching the delightful villages and small towns in the area—Fergus, Salem, West Montrose and Elora—and to locate particular sections of the gorges. But the more remarkable features of these riverscapes you will not find depicted on a conventional map or aerial photograph. Many are hidden by vertical and overhanging cliffs and among thickets of vegetation. Essential clues to the development of the riverscape are only seen when you study local detail. These clues emerge in sudden changes at the river line or in the profile of a steep cliff, under shaded overhangs or in the dim recesses of small caves. And this is to consider landscape features as they appear to the eye and on a human scale. The best way to record what is there is with camera or sketch-pad in your own hand.

With that in mind, this part of the guide describes a series of viewpoints and walks along different sections of the Grand River below Elora and of Irvine Creek gorge. The numbers in the text and on the maps identify the sites and viewpoints. In keeping with a common practice, the left bank and the right bank refer to the flanks of the gorge when facing downstream.

Here, I would also add a few words about personal safety and respect for the environment. A visit to the gorges demands caution and common sense. Some relative-

Canoes in the Grand Gorge, looking downstream from below the Mill Inn, Elora.

ly safe paths follow their edges for several kilometres in the Gorge Park, managed by the Grand River Conservation Authority. At a few points, paths provide fairly easy access to the floors of the gorges. But in most places the cliffs are sheer; leave these to people with rock-climbing equipment and ability. Certain parts of the rivers—and all of them during floods—are best left to the canoeist with life jacket and whitewater experience. At all times, it is advisable to dress suitably for the season and terrain, keeping in mind that comfortable walking shoes are always essential. A winter visit requires warm clothing, strong footwear and the foresight to avoid steep, icy areas. As in all such places of natural beauty and priceless heritage, the old maxim still applies: leave only footprints, take away only memories and photographs.

Summer flows over the falls at Elora.

Three Classic Views

Three excellent viewpoints in Elora itself are accessible by road to within a few steps of the gorge. The walks between them need take no more than five or ten minutes. They provide classic scenes of the riverscape and fine overviews of the gorge features described above. If you can spare only a little time, or if you have limited mobility, you can still view these attractive panoramas from the edge of the Grand and Irvine gorges.

• S I T E   1 •
T H E   F A L L S   A N D
I S L E T   R O C K

Beside the Mill Inn at Elora, the Grand River swirls around Islet Rock and plunges abruptly into the main gorge, where it enters a cluster of large reef masses. They loom over the threshold of the gorge like stone guardians and overhang its first reach. This is a zone of sharp changes in the nature of the rock. The river descends into the gorge over thin-bedded material. However, the rock becomes more massive and unbroken downstream. In fact, before the river was able to cut back through the reefs to create the present falls, most or all of the flow ran eastward. A broad valley, now dry but for occasional swamps, follows the east side of the Elora Gorge Park for some two kilometres, before swinging back in a great loop to cross the line of the Grand River.

Islet Rock is also known as the "Tooth of Time." Notice how dangerously it is perched above the cataract. Looking along the line of the river's current, you see just how narrow the base is and how daring the outward flare of the platform that supports its little grove of cedars and wild flowers above. This upper part consists of a strong protective cap of reef material that gives way to thinner-bedded rock below. Captain William Gilkison, who named and founded

Elora in 1832, at first wanted to build a bridge right at the head of the falls, using the islet. Later he was persuaded to change his mind, and charged others to leave it untouched. Since then it has served as the symbol Elora, and has appeared for many years on our official emblem. Several times, local people have intervened to save or strengthen Islet Rock. You can see, on the upstream side, a buttress of concrete to protect it against the battering of floods and ice in the spring break-up.

The overhanging form of Islet Rock seems extreme because it is an island and comparatively small. Yet its flanks have profiles that you will find to be typical of many parts of the gorges. Across from the Mill Inn, a higher promontory bulges out over the stream in a similar way. As you turn to look down the main chasm, you notice, ranged one behind another, over-

hanging rockwalls of much greater height. The river has cut through and under the irregular reef masses that cap Islet Rock and the left-bank promontory, and that become progressively larger downstream [colour photograph 10].

The rock of the islet and flanks of the gorge contains fossil shellfish and some small corals. However, most abundant are colonies of the main reef-building organisms of the Guelph Formation, the *Stromatoporoidea*, or stroms, described more fully on pages 62–63. If you look closely at the rock cut that flanks the Elora Mill Inn parking lot, you will see a variety of fossils. The rock here seems to have formed in an area of pools sheltered by the surrounding reefs. Many fossils remain in their growth position. A few have been washed into small depressions or overturned by wave or current, perhaps when the water was troubled by tropical storms.

The bedrock channel below the falls looks deep and forbidding, even at low flow. In fact it consists mostly of a fairly flat rock terrace where anglers can wade to midstream with water barely reaching to their knees. However, from the plunge pool below the falls and on downstream are a series of deep, treacherous cuts and hidden potholes, the beginnings of a future, deeper gorge.

These potholes and the whole form of the chasm are mainly the products of erosion during floods. Even today, with part of the water held back by the Shand Dam above Fergus, the high spring flood over the falls remains a formidable sight and certainly worth a visit. A raging mass of white water, turned sharply to the right at the falls, is hurled head on against the rock buttress on the opposite bank. Part of the flow swirls in the embayment beneath the Mill Inn, scouring it smooth, part forms a whirlpool in the bay opposite, below the abandoned Elora hydroelectric plant. The main flood shoots through the narrows between the massive reef flanks, and is again deflected by the walls below. And so the pattern continues. It is these extreme conditions that do most of the sculpting of the gorge channel.

Between The Cove and Mill Inn, looking upstream along the first reach of the main Grand Gorge.

• S I T E 2 •
LOVER'S LEAP

[Colour photographs 5 and 6] Elora's village park borders the west side of the Grand and lower Irvine Creek. Where the two rivers and their gorges meet is a prominent nose of rock that juts out a good 4 metres over the river. It is called Lover's Leap to commemorate a legendary Indian princess, said to have leapt to her death here after her beloved had been killed in battle. The tale may have more to do with Victorian melodrama and attracting visitors than recalling First Nations' history!

Standing at Lover's Leap and looking up the Grand, you have a view over The Cove. It is one of the rarer wide sections of the gorge. In the ancient Guelph Sea this was an area of pools where lagoonal sediments formed. The river has been able to excavate them more easily than it has the surrounding massive reefs. *Cove* is an apt way to describe its appearance while recalling a cliffed seacoast. [See lower photograph, p. 33.]

The upper end of The Cove is closed off on both banks by reefs which lean far over the river. Upstream, the reefs enclose the narrows below the falls. Hidden among the trees at the base of the cliff on Lover's Leap side is one of the larger caves. It was opened out, almost 10 metres above present river level, where an underground stream followed a line of weakness between the reefs.

River junctions are critical places in riverscape development. Notice the bouldery debris that spreads out from the Irvine across the Grand, and the vegetated island that has formed opposite and slightly upstream. What these record are the stronger flood flows and debris transport of the free-flowing Irvine, compared to the regulated Grand. However, photographs of The Cove before the Shand Dam was completed in the 1940s reflect a quite different relation of the two streams. The Grand, as much the larger and more powerful stream, used to overwhelm the flows from the Irvine, sweeping its debris away downstream, even holding back its flows and depositing debris into its mouth. Today, the Grand has been tamed and even the spring floods are rarely allowed to overpower the Irvine.

Across from Lover's Leap, a huge reef is exposed along the last 100 metres of the Irvine and on along the Grand below the junction for about 50 metres. It extends the full height of the gorges at their junction. Directly opposite Lover's Leap, you see how this reef is undercut at river level. The overhang is as much as 6 metres, leaving a huge volume of rock unsupported except by its own internal strength. It is silent testimony to the toughness of these reefs. Notice also how the base of the reef seems to climb to the right. This records millennia of its lateral as well as vertical growth, gradually enveloping the surrounding lagoonal areas.

Sooner or later the overhanging mass will collapse, creating a barrier whose larger slabs and boulders will not be breached and cleared except by great floods. Your chances of witnessing such an event are small, but when the collapse occurs it will be another of the singular dramatic incidents that punctuate and distinguish the evolution of the gorges.

• S I T E 3 •
DAVID STREET BRIDGE

You may park your car beside the David Street Bridge, on the Elora Arena side, or walk there in five minutes from Lover's Leap. Looking down from the bridge, you see the deep slot created by Irvine Creek. Downstream, the water hugs the right bank, which forms vertical cliffs of irregular but mostly thin rock beds, with small reefs and large shell banks. By contrast, note the almost unbroken apron of rockslides along the left bank, the nearest of which force the water to the right. Previously, the stream undercut the left side, but in doing so it prepared the walls for large collapses whose boulders now protect that entire flank.

David Street Bridge and the main Irvine Creek Gorge, looking upstream from the Arena Caves (Site 6).

Successive builders have used this spot to bridge the Irvine since 1847. It is the narrowest place along the main Irvine Gorge and close to Elora. But why are the narrows here? In fact, the bridge sits upon overhanging promontories of mainly reef rock. It is also the first break in the almost continuous series of rockslides that have left their rubble down in the gorge between here and Lover's Leap. The promontories on which the bridge is anchored are parts of the rockwalls that have so far escaped the last phases of landsliding. Immediately upstream and downstream are old rockslide scars that left the gorge lips a good

12 metres farther apart. Their absence here may be to do with the bend in the gorge, rather than unusual strength of the rock. Moreover, pressure release fractures that form the back walls of the larger rockslides pass through the rock spurs on which the bridge sits.

The old caves below the left bank abutment, with dry travertine aprons beneath them, are evidence of an earlier, shallower gorge and a higher groundwater table. However, the features you see down in the Irvine Gorge from the David Street Bridge are best examined close up and will be the subject of our first walk.

WALK I
The Lower Irvine Gorge

In this first walk we descend to the floor of the Irvine gorge and its most readily accessible part. It is an ideal place, almost a field laboratory, for studying all the major features of the gorges. Most of the Guelph fossils are found here. You will discover a wide variety of organic build-ups, some of the largest reef masses and lagoonal sections with shell beds, and a spectacular development of rockslide deposits.

To reach the river, use the stone steps at the Elora village park. The walk passes first along the base of the cliff on the river's left bank to the David Street Bridge. We then return along the right bank—or you may want to paddle in the stream—as far as the junction with the Grand under Lover's Leap. *However, do not attempt this walk in winter when the steps are icy and treacherous.* By using binoculars many of the features can be observed from the paths along the edge of the gorge and the David Street Bridge.

•SITE 4•
ROCKWALLS, ROCKSLIDES AND OVERHANGING REEFS

At the bottom of the steps, but still some distance above the river, you reach the path that continues along the base of the rockwall. Pause and observe how the wall consists of quite extensive, tabular reef masses, half a metre or more thick. The steps end and the upper path winds across the head of a well-defined rockslide deposit.

This rockslide below the face is a fine example of how a block of bedrock, descending rapidly from the wall, rotated, split apart and spilled into the river. Take time to clamber over it and inspect its

geometry. In the middle section, the large tabular masses are partly separated and rotated so that they tilt back up the slope. Beneath the large slabs you can see rock that was much more fractured and crushed in its descent. Variations on this rockslide theme are found all the way to the David Street Bridge.

The rock face, set back just beyond the steps, is a smooth and near-vertical surface. It represents the inner wall of a *pressure release fracture* and the back wall, or breakout scar, of the rockslide below. Notice that where this smooth surface ends, a line of fracture continues *into* the rock. In fact, the form of this gorge wall, as far as the David Street Bridge, is largely defined by such release-fracture geometry.

About 40 metres beyond the steps the rockwall bulges out 3 to 5 metres. This imposing overhang is the re-excavated underside and an exposed flank of one of the larger reef masses. Close inspection will reveal interlocking colonies of *Stromatoporoids,* or stroms (see p. 62), the main organisms that built the reef.

Observe the inner flank, where a wide cleft curves in behind the overhanging rock mass. This is a tension fracture, probably due to the great weight of the outer, unsupported rock mass, which is already detached along the fracture and has slipped and tilted toward the gorge. Water and frost action are helping to weaken and open up the fracture. This is another large rockslide waiting to happen.

Think about that as you continue along the path under the overhang! Notice the notch, the undercut area which has left so great an overhanging rock mass. This landform, appropriately called a *visor*, is excavated in thinner beds and patchy growths upon which the main reef was built. Surprisingly, however, the visor lies well above present river level. It was almost certainly initiated by the river's undercutting, but suggests that when this was happening, the bed of the gorge itself was higher. Meanwhile, if the undercutting is largely due to the river, the notch has continued to grow inward beneath the reef without the river's aid. That can be attributed to groundwater seeping out under the reef; to algae and moss

1 Fall along Irvine Creek Gorge upstream of Site 5.

2 (TOP) The falls and Islet Rock in summer. 3 (BELOW) The Grand Gorge looking upriver from The Cove toward Elora. 4 (OPPOSITE) The falls and Islet Rock in winter.

5 (*OPPOSITE*) *Lover's Leap seen from across Irvine Creek.*   6 (*THIS PAGE, TOP*) *The junction of Irvine Creek Gorge with the Grand viewed from The Cove; Lover's Leap to the right and overhanging reef mass to the left.*   7 (*BELOW*) *Irvine Creek Gorge, looking upstream from the base of the rockslide (Site 4) toward David Street Bridge.*

8 (TOP) The Stone Sidewalk (Site 23). 9 (BELOW) At the foot of Icicle Wall in winter (Site 17). 10 (OPPOSITE) The Stone Guardians. Looking downstream through the narrows below the falls at Elora (below Site 1).

11 (TOP) Overhanging reef masses, caves and travertine aprons on the left flank of Irvine Creek Gorge (near Site 4). 12 (BELOW) 'Clam bed.' A fallen block of dolostone with fossil remains of Megalomoidea canadensis *(Site 5).*

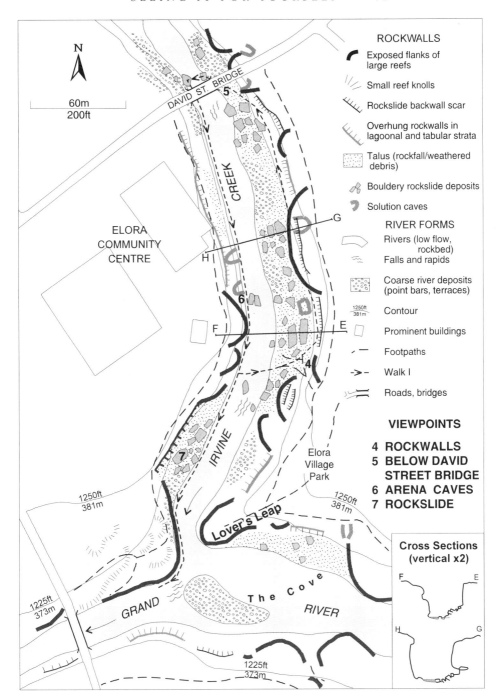

Figure 16. Walk I: a map showing the itinerary, main landform features and numbered sites along the lower Irvine Creek.

David Street Bridge and the main Irvine Gorge, looking upstream in winter.

growing on and weakening the moist rock; to winter frost; and to alternating wet and dry conditions in summer. Farther on, you also see small caves that formed at the base of the reef, where groundwater comes out, and along lines of fracture or reef edges [Colour photograph 11].

• SITE 5 •
BELOW DAVID STREET BRIDGE

The impressive 25-metre stone pillar and bridge spans help create one of the most dramatic scenes in the gorges. The pillar is built upon solid, lumpy reef rock. On the left, or north, wall the bridge rests upon an overhanging reef. Some small and now dry caves are cut in the wall beneath the reef, with old travertine deposits spilling from their mouths. You will notice, about 8 metres above river level on the other side, a "clam bed," 2 to 3 metres thick. It passes under the bridge and stretches for as much as 100 metres, and must have contained thousands of clams, specifically the large and distinctive fossil of the Guelph Formation, *Megalomoides canadensis*. On the right bank immediately upstream and downstream of the bridge, and on the left just upstream, are large rockfall blocks made up of units from the clam bed. They offer you an opportunity for a close-up view of the fossils.

You can cross to the right bank at low flow on stepping stones—blocks from former rockfalls carried here by the river. We return downstream, walking on the smoothed rocky pavement of the gorge floor. With a sharp eye, you will pick out small fossils underfoot, including shellfish and corals. Meanwhile, you pass under a steep, rough rockwall, consisting of thin-bedded inter-reef sediments and tabular growths above and below the clam bed. This ends about 100 metres downstream where two conspicuous caves open 2 to 3 metres above river level.

• SITE 6 •
THE ARENA CAVES AND OLD FOOTBRIDGE AREA

These caves mark the end of the lagoonal beds where encroaching reefs create the protruding rockwall and buttress beyond which the river turns to the right. The caves have been created by groundwater dissolving the rock along lines of weakness between and beneath the reef masses. Climbing up into either, you will also observe how they open out inside, where erosion has exploited pressure release fractures.

Just beyond the lower cave, at the base and outer part of the prominent buttress, you can see a variety of well-preserved fossils. A little below that, a footbridge used to cross the Irvine. It linked the steps where we descended from the village park to a wooden staircase going up the cut on the right bank to the arena area. You will see, downstream about 20 metres, two concrete piers on their side in the water and stranded against the right and left banks. They used to support the bridge and are a small testament to the power of the floodwaters from Hurricane Hazel in 1954, which destroyed the footbridge.

Notice, too, how the sequence of rock-slides along the opposite bank comes to an end, and the river crosses to the Lover's Leap side, hugging the rockwall there. Meanwhile, for 100 metres, the right bank has a terrace of coarse river gravels, with a path on it that we follow, and an apron of rockfall debris spilling over it and making this the *inactive* cliff.

• SITE 7 •
THE ROCKSLIDE

This is the most eloquent and, as of 1995, youngest of the rotational rockslides along the lower Irvine. It represents an almost identical event and situation to that we saw at the base of the steps from the village park. The absence of mature trees lets you see it more clearly. The sheer wall from which it fell is still stained with iron from weathering and water that used to seep down along the pressure release fracture. At the base of the wall a classic rotational slide developed, with the central large blocks tilted back, those below gliding and spilling down into the river [photograph, and FIG. 14, page 32]. I am told the slide occurred in the early 1970s.

Continuing toward the Grand, you pass beneath the massive reef guarding the junction of the two streams and see how astonishing is the depth of undercutting. Note also, right at the junction, a half pot-hole smoothly rounded in the base of the reef. That records how the floods from the main Grand used to strike the wall here creating a whirlpool of enormous power. On the knolls just beyond that and beside the Grand are some good exposures of fossils of the reef builders. This is where you can observe the stony delta built by the Irvine and the "flowerpot" overhang of Lover's Leap. There is also a fine view upstream across the tranquil waters of The Cove to the falls and Mill Inn [lower photograph, page 33].

If you have been able to reach this spot, then the river flows will be low enough for you to continue on down the Grand for about one kilometre. You walk on the smoothed and scalloped rock of the gorge floor to the rockfall and overhanging reef masses opposite Site 11 (High Lookout), described in Walk II.

─ WALK II ─

The Upper Circuit of the Grand Gorge: The Falls to the Middle Bridge and Back to the Arena

This itinerary follows the Grand Gorge downstream above its left bank from the falls at Elora as far as Middle Bridge, and returns on the right bank to the junction with the Irvine [FIG. 17]. Allow at least two hours.

The walk begins on the east side of Victoria Street Bridge at the falls, which are reached by a path that dodges in behind the furniture factory. You can then proceed along paths close to the river under the road bridge and into the Elora Gorge Conservation Park. All along this side you encounter rock terraces and relict cliff lines back from the river, "ledges of rock," as John Connon described them, "in some places as wide as a street, on which trees are growing." (*Elora: The Early History of Elora and Vicinity.*) They represent old stream levels and the early complex development of the Grand Gorge.

• SITE 8 •

MILL VIEW

Standing above the falls on the path opposite Elora Mill Inn, you obtain the best view of where the main Grand gorge begins. Swallowed by a throat of stone, the river almost seems to disappear. From the weir above the falls, the water splashes over thin beds of rock that have broken away to form irregular steps. To right and left of Islet Rock, these steps steepen into a convex staircase of little ledges that form the falls.

The promontory jutting out from the left bank here, capped by more massive reef rock, forces the water to take a sharp turn to the right.

This is a formidable place when the river is in flood. The acceleration of the flow over the falls, the thunder of it beating upon the walls, will take your breath away. Boiling plumes of spray, rising above the maelstrom, are visible long before the falls come into view. In cold weather they frost the trees and walls with coats of rime.

Here are many vestiges of the past industrial uses of this site of water power. Upstream, there is a fine view of Elora's riverfront. The old flume leading to Elora's abandoned Hydro plant runs along this side of the river, bypassing the falls. Before leaving this site, step down into the dry, lower section of the flume and walk to where the concrete lining ends. There are good exposures of the colonial organisms that built the reefs. The irregular, domed and ball-like growths have weathered out like gnarled tree stumps. Individual colonies may exceed 10 centimetres vertically and 30 or more laterally. Many are joined together in tabular units or beds. The higher ones tend to be more massive. In the walls of the old stilling pool at the end of the flume, you see these give way to successively thinner beds. This sequence is similar to that of Islet Rock and helps explain its unusual shape.

Between Sites 8 and 9 lies wooded terrain with rocky knolls and depressions, cut in low reefs of the kind just described, and the emerging crowns of the much larger reefs that loom over the gorge. The walls in this section consist of spectacular overhanging promontories and smoothly rounded bays, drilled out by the river in strong, massive rock.

• SITE 9 •

THE CUT AND THE COVE

About 100 metres into the woods, a narrow gully in the rock, The Cut, slants diagonally down to river level, ending on a small

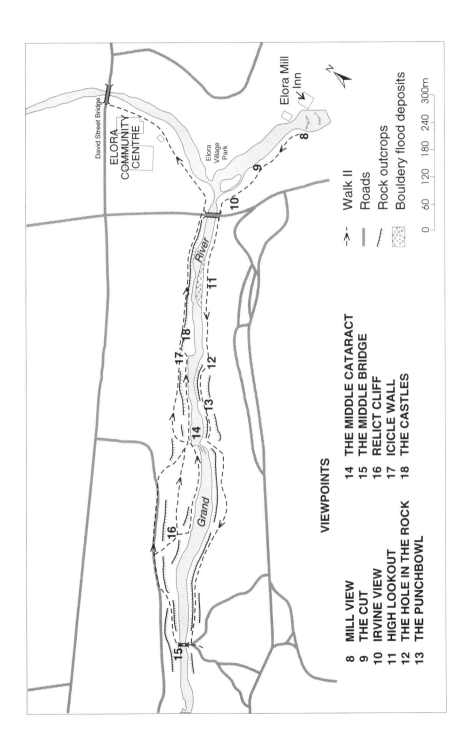

Figure 17. Walk II: a map showing the itinerary, main landform features and numbered sites along the upper main Grand Gorge.

Rockwall with exposed reefs and rockfall as seen from High Lookout (Site 11).

gravel beach between overhanging cliffs. From here you have excellent views over The Cove toward Lover's Leap. Except in flood, the wide, tranquil waters are a restful change from the falls and gloomy chasm below them. You see how The Cove, described more fully above as seen from Lover's Leap (Site 2), is overlooked in all directions by the bulging flanks of large reefs. The one immediately upstream of The Cut is one of the most astonishing overhangs in the whole gorge.

• SITE 10 •
IRVINE VIEW

Returning to the path above the gorge and just beyond The Cut, you obtain the best view over and into the junction of the Irvine. You see how it breaches and undercuts the large reef to enter The Cove through narrows whose walls lean dangerously toward each other. The bouldery delta has been left by floods, flushing the

coarse fragments through the narrows only to drop them where the current slows and spreads into The Cove.

Between Sites 10 and 11, the path continues under the highway bridge and into the Conservation Authority's Elora Gorge Park. To the left of the path are low stone benches recording ancient high levels of erosion. The massive reefs give way to tabular and lagoonal beds for about 150 metres, and the sheer gorge walls are parallel, forming a deep, moody and remarkably straight trough.

• SITE 11 •
THE HIGH LOOKOUT

This viewpoint at the edge of the gorge, with a stone wall to lean on, provides an excellent opportunity to take stock of the scale and features of the deeper parts of the gorge. Carefully scan the gorge walls opposite. You will notice another set of massive reefs etched out in cream-coloured overhangs. A little downstream, below the reefs, a large rockfall forms a natural breakwater that guides the current toward the left or east bank.

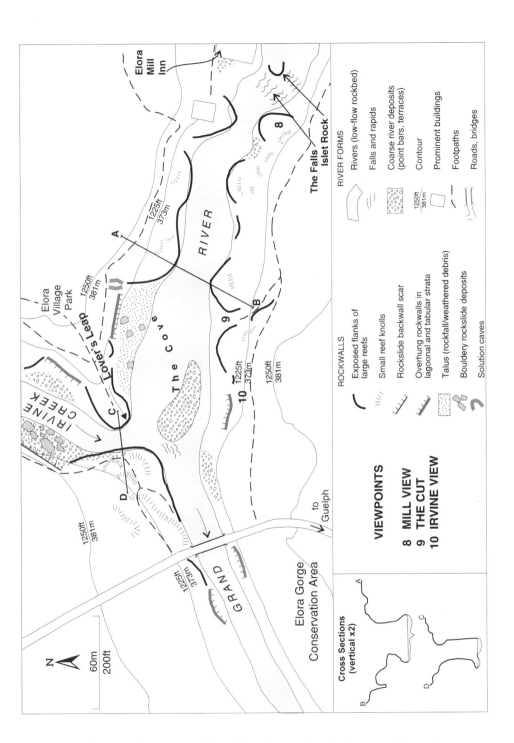

Figure 18. Walk II: map showing detailed landform features along the first part of the walk.

• SITE 12 •

THE HOLE IN THE ROCK

About 200 metres farther along the path at the edge of the gorge, you encounter steps that suddenly disappear into the earth like gates of Hades. Going down them, you pass beneath a shadow-filled stone arch. Pause in here to let your eyes get used to the dim light, or, if you have a flashlight, begin at once to scan the roof and walls. This is an unusually good place to see clean and fairly well-preserved fossils of the stroms (*Stromatoporoids*), interspersed with small, elegant colonies of corals (*Tabulates*). There are a few clusters of lamp shells (*Brachiopods*), some a little larger than golf balls, mostly showing the cast of the body inside the shell (see p. 60–61).

The natural arch looks down upon a rock terrace representing an earlier river level, which you reach by wooden steps. Looking back, you see that the Hole in the Rock has a small companion cave. This is the famous Wampum Cave where relics were found in 1880 by two Elora schoolboys, students of David Boyle's. He followed up by excavating the cave. Apparently the relics were left by a party of Neutral Indians fleeing the wars of the late seventeenth century, but the cave has the attributes of sacred caves the world over, and may have been known to them long before.

Typically, the cave and natural arch open up between two distinct units of rock and along vertical breaks. The upper unit, whose fossils we inspected in the Hole in the Rock, consists of a thick carapace of reef, much like that seen earlier near the falls. Below are dense, finer grained, tabular beds. When the gorge floor was nearer this level, ground water came to the surface along the division to help form caves.

Out from the arch is a large rockslide of the upper, reefy strata, where an overhang collapsed. The cliff and rock terrace are part of a whole series of well-defined *relict cliffs* that occur on this side, recording the tangled history of downcutting and migration of the gorge toward the right, or west, flank.

• SITE 13 •

THE PUNCHBOWL

The Punchbowl, about 80 metres farther on, lies just off the path, above the river. Easily missed, it is a bowl-shaped depression in the rock, roughly 40 metres across. It seems that a substantial stream, or perhaps overflowing flood waters, once came this way. A waterfall plunged over the lip and drove the flow in a wide circle. The rim of the bowl is overhung by the same fossil-rich reef beds that cap the Hole in the Rock. The northern flank, a smoothly rounded bowl-form, is another good place to find stroms and corals. I have found one tabulate coral colony here that is almost half a metre in diameter.

• SITE 14 •

THE MIDDLE CATARACT, OR LITTLE FALLS

A few steps farther downstream lies a bare platform of rock jutting out above the river where it rushes over the Middle Cataract, sometimes called the Little Falls. These are hardly falls, though the water dashes through at a great pace, roiling and churning into a narrow cut on the left side, even at low flow. Below the cataract, which is enclosed and floored by reefs, the river opens out into a wide section flanked by lagoonal beds, before it plunges into a further narrows.

The viewpoint itself is the crown of a reef similar to that which forms the resistant tread of the cataract and the head of the Hole in the Rock. It rewards a careful look for the honeycombs and chains of coral colonies. Stroms form the main mass. More will be said of the Middle Cataract when we reach it from the other side.

• SITE 15 •
THE MIDDLE BRIDGE

The last 250 metres of path to the Middle Bridge are on a rock bench recording another higher old level of the gorge. With a small matching bench on the other side, it provides the foundation for the bridge. Here the river has recently been slicing through massive tabular beds and reefs to create the narrowest part of the main Grand gorge. This is an ideal bridging point. In the mid-nineteenth century a tree lay across it, known as the Indian Bridge. A photograph showing it in 1860 appears in John Connon's *Elora: The Early History of Elora and Vicinity*.

The bridge allows us to cross the river and return to Elora on the right bank. On that side, the walk has several distinct sections, the first of which takes us from the Middle Bridge back to the Middle Cataract. This reach is also affected by old levels and migrations of the gorge. It is a tumbled country of relict cliff lines and rock benches. You will find that the paths down to the river near the Middle Cataract are easy and scenically rewarding.

• SITE 16 •
RELICT CLIFF

About 250 metres along the park road, up from the Middle Bridge, you can descend a narrow path through the trees to the right. It goes down to and under a low, relict cliff line with overhanging slabs. An old level of the gorge, the cliff preserves its steepness and provides a sheltered spot. It can be delightfully warm and sunny through the morning and middle of the day, even in winter. Here there appears to have been an inter-reef area, with beds of variable thickness full of vugs. Notice the typical ramp of weathered debris, a little out from the cliff and sloping down to the swampy terrace at the old gorge level. It represents centuries of weathering and small rockfalls that have helped wear back the cliff.

From here you have several choices of route. You can continue at this level or return to the road above. You can also go directly down to the river, where there are remains of a rough stone lane made when this was part of the farm above. It is the only place between Salem or Elora and the end of the main gorge where thirsty cattle could safely get down to the Grand for a drink. Each of these routes can be used to continue upriver and reach the Middle Cataract.

• SITE 14 •
THE MIDDLE CATARACT AGAIN

Except at flood time, this is a place where the floor of the gorge can be readily examined. It lies hemmed in by a system of reefs. The cataract itself tumbles over others at deeper levels, whose lumpy crowns you can walk over. In the low cliffs on this side many fossils are exposed. There are excellent examples of a characteristic coral of the Guelph, *Flecheria* (called *Picnostylus* in older texts).

Upstream from the Middle Cataract, the main cliff is high and sheer, but the country above is complicated by rock gullies and potholes cut through a system of large reefs. They record the work of several old, dry tributary channels and a present-day stream. One explanation of the many old levels and shifting directions of the gorge in this area is that the main Grand originally joined the Irvine here, coming in a great sweep from the east side. You can find evidence that other streams, now abandoned, came in from both sides.

Exercising caution, during low flows it is well worth proceeding upstream on the gorge floor. The route passes under some massive overhanging reef flanks, undercut at river level where spring lines and travertine aprons are found. Halfway along, a tributary enters in a small waterfall. You will see that it has cut down along a line of fractures that sever the reef and continue

• SITE 17 •
THE ICICLE WALL

About 200 metres upstream of the Middle Cataract, is a high, recessed vertical wall with overhanging cornice at the head. Drenched by springs that emerge near the top, it is quite impressive in summer but in winter it is truly magnificent. After a few days of heavy frost, it is covered from top to base with huge icicles and great beehives of ice. [Photograph on p. 65; colour photograph 9.] Beyond this wall you can ascend a steep path into the area of The Castles.

• SITE 18 •
THE CASTLES

The gorge walls here actually break up into a series of high towers from halfway above the river. They are separated from each other by old channels and potholes where abandoned streams once entered the gorge. The towers and knolls are formed in the more resistant cores of reefs. There are plenty of strom colonies exposed in the walls, corals in some places, and many small caves and hidden overhangs. It is a place to take time to scramble around and was a favourite haunt of my children. Each of them would adopt one of the high reef knolls as her "castle," to defend it or invite the others over for a picnic.

across the bed of the river into the far wall. This is a true geological fault, the result of earth movements breaking the strata, not of reef-settling or erosion. It is one of the few faults to affect the gorge rocks. In this area also, out in the river, you can see active potholes and how some of them join up to form a deeper cut that wanders down the centre of the channel.

The large reef ends abruptly with caves in its upstream flank, from which springs and large, vegetated travertine aprons descend. The rockfall boulders at this place are worth inspecting. They contain some of the best-preserved examples of larger tabulate coral colonies. There is an opportunity to see the honeycomb and chain patterns because the corals are cut and polished at various angles [see p. 63]. There are also good examples of stroms and *Brachiopods* mixed with the corals. The rockfall descended from the underside of the wide cornice overhead at the start of the Icicle Wall.

From Site 18 almost to the junction of the Irvine with the Grand is a long uninterrupted sheer cliff to the river. Higher than that opposite, and with few indications of the old gorge levels, it continues to the road bridge. Trees line and lean over the edge. Sudden glimpses of the deep trough of the Grand appear beneath your feet, where the path skirts the edge. The road bridge marks the end of the Conservation Park. Beyond it is again a complicated terrain representing old river levels and shifting channels above Site 7 and the Irvine junction.

WALK III
The Lower Circuit of the Grand Gorge: The Middle Bridge to the Low Bridge and Back

Along this majestic lower section of the main Grand gorge you will see striking differences between the right and left banks. The right bank is almost everywhere a single vertical or overhanging wall. Only minor signs of old river levels are visible, mostly in the wooded country back from the gorge lip. Under these northward-facing cliffs it is generally more humid, if not positively soggy. You will find many more springs and more vegetation, including the most extensive developments of the "travertine gardens." Even on sunny days there is a cool green or bluish light.

By contrast, much of the left bank is stepped, with old river levels and relict cliff lines. Under the cedar trees the floor is often dry and bare. For plant growth, the greater sunshine hours of the southward-facing slopes are offset by their droughtiness. Many sections of the low cliffs do not intersect the permanent water table, and therefore lack springs. But there are some convenient places to walk down to the river bank and out on the flood-deposited boulder bars. A dense growth of vegetation covers the bars in summer.

Our itinerary begins and ends at Site 15, the Middle Bridge, and proceeds first down the east side to the Low Bridge, and returns along the other bank of the Grand. It can be done comfortably in a couple of hours, but it is worth allowing more time. To see conditions below and above the cliffs, you may have to double back where river-level paths end in sheer cliffs.

• SITE 19 •
THE SECOND COVE

Below the Middle bridge lies an interesting country of more pronounced rock terraces and old cliff lines. You can proceed along the lowest rock terrace for some 200 meters, from just below where the road climbs up from the bridge. Here are increasingly high and overhanging relict cliffs that give a small foretaste of the Stone Sidewalks farther down. Notice the slabs of dolostone that have fallen from the undersides of cornice-type overhangs. Along much of the cliff base is the typical ramp of rockfall and smaller weathered debris that has built up since the river was at this level, and a dip between it and the rockwall [see photograph on p. 54].

The cliffs mark the deepening and westward migration of the gorge. In this section, the river passes from the narrow, steep canyon below the Middle Bridge into a very wide reach of the main gorge that can appropriately be called the Second Cove. This marks a transition from massive reef rock into more readily excavated inter-reef beds. Here is a wide pool, reflecting the far cliffs upon its smooth surface. Then the river swings away to undercut the far wall, while across the mouth of the pool is the largest boulder bar yet encountered.

About 170 metres below the Middle Bridge you can descend to river level, using caution, down a steep, smooth embayment in the cliffs. Usually dry in summer, but wet or ice-covered at other times, it was once a cataract where another lost river used to enter the gorge. On the gorge floor, between the great boulder bar and the cliff, are some large rockfalls that helped steer the river toward the far bank. On the boulder bar itself, notice the crude natural stacking of the stones, carried into place and forced together in former floods. The boulder bar pinches out downstream as the river swings back towards the left-

The Cascade from Site 21.

bank cliff, which becomes a single sheer rock wall. Unless you are up to wading or rock climbing, you must go back up the dry cataract.

Over the next 400 metres or so, the gorge achieves its grandest scale, the walls enclosing a wide, deep trough. There are dizzying glimpses across the chasm between you and the far walls. The river rushes against the base of the cliff far below your feet. The main flow has evidently followed the left bank for many decades, if not centuries. That is shown by the broad, old river bars covered in tall trees along the right side of the gorge floor.

• SITE 20 •

THE LITTLE WATERFALL

A true waterfall is made by the stream that is dammed to form a small artificial lake in the Conservation Park. There is only a small notch in the cliff before the water plunges down onto rockfall boulders and dead tree trunks. These seem to recall the fiercer action of floods before the stream was dammed. This is a good place to appreciate the character of the rock walls. About 5 metres below the lip of the falls is another of the fossil clam beds, with large casts and moulds of *Megalamoides* decorating the cliff face.

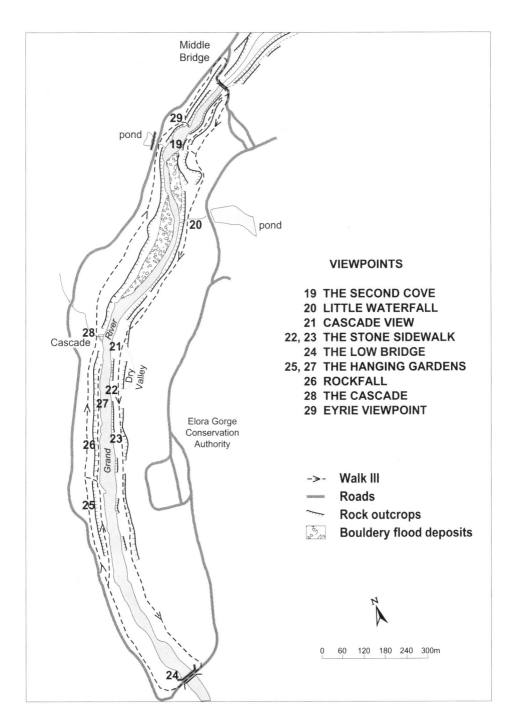

Figure 19. Walk III: a map showing the itinerary, main landform features and numbered sites along the lower main Grand Gorge.

•SITE 21•

THE DRY VALLEY
AND CASCADE VIEW

About 150 metres beyond the Little Water-fall, another dry canyon descends in a series of steps almost parallel to the Grand, before swinging to the right and giving easy access to river level. If you continue out onto the bouldery river bar, there is a fine view of The Cascade tumbling down the cliff directly opposite. The curtain of white water splits into skeins and rivulets over an irregular staircase of stone steps about 20 metres high.

•SITES 22 AND 23•

THE STONE SIDEWALKS

The Stone Sidewalks comprise dry path-ways beneath relict limestone walls over a distance of more than a kilometre. Along much of their length the paths are shel-tered beneath wide cornices of over-hanging rock, broad enough to keep the rain off on wet days. The paths run close to the cliff. On their riverward side is a fallen mess of boulders and weathered debris descending to a rock terrace below. There are occasional great slabs of rock that dropped from the underside of the over-hanging cornices. The rockwalls are cut mostly in very massive reefs, and you can pick out lots of strom colonies in them. The cornice typically consists of a distinct tabu-lar layer that was built over the underlying thicker reef masses.

These natural "sidewalks" usually lie on the first main bench above the river. Above the cliff that leans over them is a tumbled wooded country with other relict cliff lines and reef knolls. They gradually subside southward to the flats near the Low Bridge.

• SITE 24 •
THE LOW BRIDGE

The Conservation Park road crosses this bridge—actually, more of a low causeway that is awash at higher river flows. Downstream, rock outcrops become rarer, and soon the Guelph dolostone is entirely buried beneath glacial and alluvial deposits. The valley opens out into wide, flower-strewn river flats, framed by tree-covered slopes, that continue to Inverhaugh. This part of the riverscape is a lovely prospect in all seasons, but especially when spring flowers are in bloom, or when fall colours splash the woods with crimson and gold. Later, you could obtain good views of that scene by taking the road that continues from David Street in Elora to West Montrose. Our gorge walk returns upstream along the west side of the Grand.

This flank consists mostly of a single main cliff down to the river, often hidden by large trees growing above and at its base. You will encounter occasional rugged areas of reef knolls along the top of the cliff. Its base is almost one continuous *visor* overhung by reef rock. Below Second Cove it is only rarely reached by the river. Aprons of bouldery debris sloping down to the water, or onto intermittent, treed river bars, reflect a long period as inactive cliff.

• SITES 25 AND 27 •
THE HANGING GARDENS

Beginning about 150 metres upstream of the Low Bridge and continuing almost to the Second Cove, the cliff base supports long sections of living travertine aprons. They can be visited at the two sites marked on the map by descending from above, but if you follow the path under the cliff they will be almost continuously at your side. Sheltered beneath overhanging rock and rarely visited, they form undisturbed hanging gardens of mosses, interspersed with herbs, sedges, wild flowers and small ferns, and watered by springs. Their growth marries rock, groundwater and plant life in a special kind of ecology, uniquely well-developed here.

Mosses drape the steepest parts of the hanging gardens, bright green in spring, fading to mottled browns and dull greens in summer and fall. They are fringed below by a brilliant apron of bright green ferns that turn yellow and then brown in fall. These are strange, misty places raised a little above the river and lost among trees. In most places they are illuminated only by indirect sunlight reflected from the river and far cliffs. Yet they seem to glow with an inner brightness and sparkling haloes of water droplets. There is an elfin light about the "gardens," strangely luminous beneath the shade of brooding cliffs and dark cedars.

• SITE 26 •
ROCKFALL

There are numerous rockfalls at river level, which have descended from the sheer west-bank cliffs. However, at this site you can observe a fairly large and fresh example. It actually consists of at least two events, the latest of which occurred in the spring of 1988, when it smashed through bushes and trees to reach the river. The large slabs fell from the flank and underside of an overhanging reef mass. The fallen rock contains numerous fossils.

Beyond the large rockfall, the path below the cliff soon gives out and you must retrace your steps to near Site 25, where you can scramble up a rocky cut to the top of the cliff. Between here and The Cascade is wooded country with narrow paths along the cliff edge, and occasional small breaks where you can look out over the river. For much of the way, the country beside the gorge consists of outcrops of more massive

reefs, carved by ice and the pre-gorge river flows into distinctive knolls and irregular depressions between them.

• SITE 28 •
THE CASCADE

A small stream wending its way out of the rolling farmland west of the gorge abruptly tumbles down the cliff face. While we had our best view of it from Site 21, it is interesting to explore the Cascade stream on this side. You will see how the shallow bedrock channel steepens over small rock steps before plunging down into the gorge. The rock is rather scraggy, broken and eroded into the small, irregular steps that give The Cascade its special character. Indications are that it was once a more substantial stream. Eroded areas on either side suggest a wider cascade or greater flood action in the past.

From here to the Second Cove are many wet places where springs and intermittent streams emerge inland from the cliff edge. Looking down at the base of the latter you see the old tree-covered boulder bars and, on the far side, the steep cliff hugged by the river. Above the Second Cove on this side lies a small artificial pond. Its outlet stream forms another small waterfall after being confined to a culvert under the road, which comes to the edge of gorge here.

• SITE 29 •
EYRIE VIEWPOINT

Before following the road to complete the circuit back to the Middle Bridge, take a moment to enjoy one last spectacular view. A narrow path curves along the edge of the promontory that closes off the upstream flank of the Second Cove. At its extreme tip you step from the trees to gain an eagle's-eye view out over the cove and on down this section where Grand gorge achieves its greatest scale. It is, perhaps, the most breathtaking view anywhere along the gorges.

Lover's Leap as seen from below.

THE LIFE OF THE ELORA GORGE:

ITS FOSSILS AND ITS PEOPLE

Guelph Life: A Guide to the Fossils

Elora sometime since started a public museum....To give some idea of the curiosities of nature presented to the Elorians, we have only to name echinus, *a* Megalomus compressus—*specimens of* Heliophylum Halli, Zaphrentes prolifica, Orthis livia, Spirifer, Mediolopsis modiolaris, Ambatychia radiata, Orthoceras, Stenopora fibrosa *and* echinoid erecta. *Such trifles may do to begin with, but of course, something more rare must be procured to keep up any permanent interest in the "show."*
The Elora *Lightning Express*, June 12, 1874

David Boyle, curator of the museum described here, would have been the first to enjoy the reporter's tongue-in-cheek remarks. But some of those jaw-cracking Latin names do refer to the greatest treasures in Boyle's collection; fossils that he and his pupils had gathered in Elora Gorge.

Some 150 species of fossil have been identified in our area, many of them first unearthed in or around the gorges. A few got their names from local places, or from personalities like Boyle who found them [see p. 63]. You will enjoy the gorges all the more if you can recognize some of the fossils and know a little about the habits of the original organisms. A good field guide to

fossils is always useful for the landscape explorer. Unfortunately, there is not one that covers the particular examples around Elora. After all, we are looking at a special and short-lived episode in the history and geography of life. Meanwhile, most of the research on the fossils here is 60 years old or more.

The Silurian Period occurred in the Palaeozoic, or ancient life era. It marked the end of the Lower Palaeozoic when life had largely developed in the sea. Marine limestones like the gorge rocks, created by organisms living in shallow seas, made major contributions to the geological record. Fascinating in themselves, the fossils also provide you with clues to the arrangement of reefs and pools. Here I will introduce some typical fossils, suggesting what to look for in order to find them, and how they reveal the secrets of that reef-strewn sea floor. In the reference material at the end of this book I recommend further sources to help anyone who wants to learn more.

Plant life must have been the most abundant living matter in the Guelph Sea. It served, as always, to feed most of the other creatures. But its remains are hard to recognize, including traces of the mats of algae that must have coated much of the lagoons and reef flanks. The easiest fossils to find are of marine animals, especially shellfish.

FOSSIL SHELLFISH

*Almost all the children in the village upwards
of five or six years of age, can distinguish*
Megalomus Canadensis, *quite as readily
as they can an Early Rose potato or
a Swedish turnip.*
David Boyle, On the Local Geology of Elora (1874)

If there were space travellers 400 million years ago, the Guelph Sea reefs might have provided them with excellent stops for seafood cookouts. Much of what they would have found were ancient relatives of today's edible shellfish [FIG. 20]. You can find for yourself long-extinct relatives of clams and oysters, known to paleontology, the science of ancient life, as *Bivalves.* There are whelks, periwinkles, sea snails and conchs, members of the *Gastropods*; and forebears of cuttlefish and the elegant nautilids, the *Cephalopods.*

These are all related within the great life group or *phylum* of the molluscs, which take their name from the Latin word *mollis*, meaning "soft-bodied." What you find in gorges, however, is their hard parts—casts and moulds of their shells referred to by scientists as *valves.*

The largest of the shelled species is the most readily discovered fossil, the bivalve *Megalomoidea canadensis*, an extinct relative of today's clams [FIG. 20]. Following his geological explorations of 1849 and 1850, the Provincial Geologist, Alex Murray, reported that "this shell...was seen in greatest abundance at Galt [now Cambridge] and at Elora, on the Grand River, associated with numerous other organic remains." It used to be called *Megalomus* or *Megalamus canadensis*. By the 1870s, if David Boyle's teaching was as good as he believed, most schoolchildren in Elora could recognize and name it. We may proceed, suitably humbled.

This clam appeared shortly before the Guelph time and suffered extinction at its end, thus making it a characteristic fossil of the Guelph Formation. It is found throughout the gorge area, sometimes clustered in large numbers. Individuals are usually 10 to 20 centimetres long. The shell form, with its two heart-shaped valves and ribbed exterior, may be clearly visible. Often, however, it is poorly preserved. All you see is a mould of the meaty body, like a large stone plum; or no more than an airfoil-shaped hieroglyphic etched into a rockwall, where one valve has been dissolved away.

Although these clams are found in a wide variety of settings, they favoured sheltered lagoons or inter-reef areas. In such places, if you discover one, you will usually detect lots of them. In some cases you see countless individuals massed like fruit in an oversize plum cake. These clam beds, in which bodies and shells accumulated along with the sediment they helped to trap, have left some extensive units of limestone.

The clams may be among the larger, more easily discovered fossils, but they lack the elegance of some others. The coiled shells of the *Gastropods*, for example, can be distinctly handsome. Over 60 species have been identified in the Guelph Formation of Ontario, most between one and three centimetres in diameter. Often you will find them where the rock has fractured along the outer surface of the shell to reveal its spiral form. At times the growth lines can be distinguished, dividing the rounded whorls. Some shells are squat, some globose and a few high spired. Among the high spired is *Murchisonia boylei*, named after the persistent David Boyle. Local places supply the names of other species, including *Lophospira elora* and *Holopea guelphensis.*

Other molluscs belong to the class of *Cephalopods* (pronounced *seff*alopods). We know of about 20 large and small species here. Moreover, it has been said that Cephalopods are often the most intelligent and agile of the molluscs. Their shell forms take many shapes. Some are coiled and you need to be careful not to confuse these with the Gastropods. Those with a straight tube-like shell such as *Michelinoceras*—formerly *Orthoceras*—are easiest to identify [FIG. 20]. *Discosorus* makes a nice discovery too, its

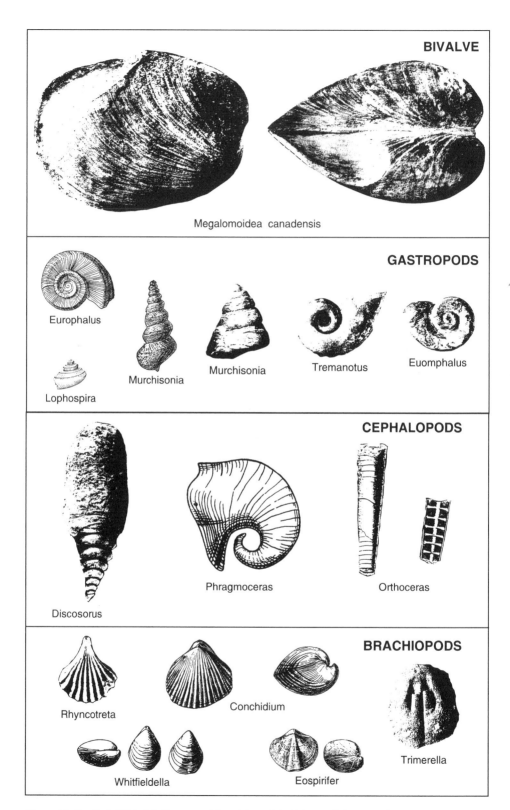

*Figure 20. Fossil shellfish (*Mollusca *and* Brachiopoda*) of the Guelph Formation.*

internal mould rather like an ice-cream cone loaded with three scoops. Sometimes all you will see is a large, smooth fragment, curved like the hilt of an old pistol or ivory-handled cane. This is the internal mould of the creature's living chamber. Lines may be incised around one end, recording the series of chambers, diminishing toward the narrow end.

But let us not leave the Cephalopods without mentioning the wondrous *Vaginoceras*. She is described as having "endo-cones within the siphuncle, and long septal neck." A very few survived the rigours of the Ordovician to grace the Silurian of New York state. Could it be that one or two came hunting amid the reefs of our area or were swept away to be stranded here in tropical storms? The visitor who discovers one of these tantalizing beasts in the gorges will outdo the famous finds made by David Boyle's pupils. Keep an eye open, but be careful! *Vaginoceras* was a predator, and the largest of all these ancient life forms, a Paleozoic sea monster that could reach 9 metres in length, a distant relative of the giant squid.

Other typical shellfish of the Guelph belong to another phylum, the *Brachiopods*. It includes the lamp shells. Of more than 30 species identified in the Guelph of Ontario, most are to be found in the gorge area. Expect to encounter examples as small as the nail on your little finger or as big as a hen's egg. Most lamp shells preferred shallow, sheltered areas. Like the clams, they obtained food from the sea water and particles of nourishment suspended in it. They lived burrowed in the lime mud, their food-gathering organ emerging from a small hole, sucking and blowing for all it was worth. You can sometimes see the lamp shells lined up along or just below a break in the strata which made up the sea-floor surface at that time.

Among predators of the Silurian you will have a better chance of finding than *Vaginoceras* are remains of the *Euripterids*, distant relatives of the scorpion. Euripterids belong to the *Arthropods*, the phylum which contains spiders, centipedes and crabs. Two species have been found in the gorge area. One, *Euripterus boylei*, commemorates the indefatigable Mr. Boyle.

FRAME BUILDERS

Corals in considerable variety may be picked up almost anywhere, and singular as it may appear, even a sponge.
David Boyle, *On the Local Geology of Elora* (1874)

Foremost among the organisms responsible for the rigid architecture of the reefs was a group of long-extinct creatures called *Stromatoporates*, or *Stromatoporoidea*. Some people say *stromatoporoid*, others *stromatoporoid*. Take your pick. Both are rather a mouthful, so let's use a short form, *stroms*.

Stroms, or their colonies, were enormously important in the Paleozoic. By volume of identifiable remains and influence they are the outstanding fossils of the gorge area. A distinguished Ontario paleontologist, Dr. William Arthur Parks, founder of the fossil collections in the Royal Ontario Museum, published a description and catalogue of the Guelph stroms in 1907, the only one of its kind as far as this author is aware. It is still not even certain where the stroms belong in the classes of life forms. Recent studies put them in the sponges, but a case may still be made for having them as relatives of the corals. It takes a specialist to differentiate among the several hundred species, but you, through careful observation, will soon begin to recognize a range of characteristic forms.

What the naked eye finds is the remains of colonies that vary in size from just a few centimetres to more than a metre across, and assume a wide variety of forms [FIG. 21]. Most are compact, rounded or dome-shaped masses, or mattress-like sheets. The name *stromatoporoid* translates literally as *porous layered*, or, if you like, *bedspread full of holes*. Strange how the commonplace words of classical Greece have

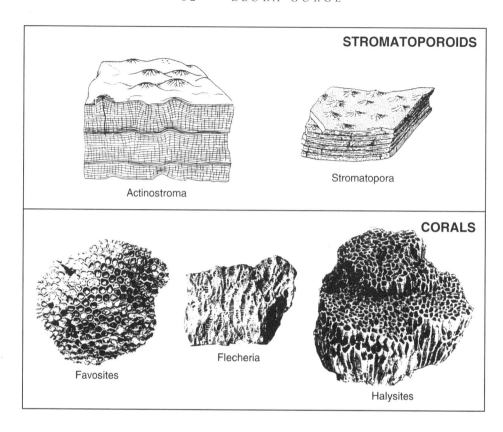

STROMATOPOROIDS

Actinostroma

Stromatopora

CORALS

Favosites

Flecheria

Halysites

Opposite page, top: Figure 21. Examples of the stroms and corals of the Guelph Formation. Below: Stromatoporoid *(strom) colony weathered in gorge wall.*

such a weighty, official feel in the hands of modern science!

Often what you may see is something resembling a cut-away cross-section of a calcified cabbage. Smaller stroms, located in vertical rockwalls, look like the open face of a sliced onion. When well preserved, the colonies may have silhouettes like intricate crochet work. In most places, only the crudest moulds or lumpy shapes survive, odd dumplings of stone exposed beneath an overhanging reef. The colonies forming the most massive reefs are usually so completely fused together and recrystallized in the change to dolomite that you can easily overlook them. The forms may show up only as faint discolouration left by weathering processes or in the uneven growth of lichens or algae over the surface. In cold, foggy weather in winter, hoar frost may form on the faintly raised areas to reveal a strom colony like an invisible writing.

The corals found in the gorges include some of the most beautiful of all the fossils. As David Boyle says, they are numerous and widespread, but you must develop an eye for finding them. They are easily missed. Many are revealed by no more than fairy shadings and fretwork that merge almost imperceptibly with other patterns in the rock. As you become familiar with the forms, your eye will pick them out with growing confidence.

There are both solitary and colonial corals, the commonest and more easily discovered being the "honeycomb" or "chain" corals [FIG. 21]. A transverse section shows off the honeycomb pattern, a vertical one the chains. A few may form quite large units. I know of one colony of *Halysites* almost a metre across, with 75 centimetres of vertical growth. Most of the Guelph corals preferred fairly sheltered locations and are often found interspersed with stroms, or encrusting them.

This only begins to introduce the range of fossils you may encounter. For those who wish to go deeper, the reference materials at the end should help. Some idea of the riches still to be explored is given by a list of those fossils that acquired their names from local or nearby sites and local residents.

SELECTED GUELPH FORMATION FOSSILS NAMED FROM LOCATIONS IN SOUTHERN ONTARIO, OR (*) INDIVIDUALS WHO WORKED IN THE GORGE AREA.

The list is based on the Royal Ontario Museum's collection (courtesy of Dr. Janet Waddington, Paleontology Department).

Class Stromatoporoidea
  Stromatopora galtensis
  Stromatoporella elora
  Stromatoporella elora
    minuta
  Hermatostroma guelphica
  Labechia durhamensis
Class Anthozoa
  Favosites niagrensis
  Flecheria guelphensis

Phylum Brachiopoda
  Monomorella durhamensis
  Rhinobolus galtensis
  Eospirifer niagrensis
Class Bivalvia
  Megalomoides canadensis
  Iliona canadensis
  Prolucina galtensis
Class Gastropoda
  Archinacella canadensis
  Pleurotomaria townsendi *
  Euomphalus galtensis
  Euomphalopteris elora
  Lophospira hespelerensis
  Lophospira guelphica
  Lophospira conradi *

  Lophospira elora
  Eotomaria durhamensis
  Eotomaria galtensis
  Hormotoma whiteavesi
  Turritoma boylei *
  Poleumita durhamensis
  Holopea guelphensis
  Diaphorostoma niagrense
Class Cephalopoda
  Ascoceras townsendi *
  Orthoceras brucensis
Class Ostracoda
  Leperditia phaseolus guelphica
  Leperditia balthica guelphica
Subclass Eurypterida
  Euripterus boylei *

People in the Landscape

Had there been no river, offering the promise of water-power for driving mills, and with its tributary streams watering the nearby valleys, there would have been no village and the founders would have looked elsewhere for a townsite.

Hugh Templin, *Fergus: The Story of a Little Town* (1933)

The memories and moods of a thousand rivers move through Canada's history. The First Peoples had been travelling along those rivers and living beside them for millennia. European exploration and settlement also followed the water courses. Many Ontario towns grew up at sites of river crossings or the junction of waterways. Elora and Salem mark places where it is easier to bridge and tap the streams above the gorge sections, and where the fall of water into the main gorges has provided power.

Just when the first human eyes gazed upon the Upper Grand, and whose eyes they were, remains uncertain. The cautious view has the peopling of North America begin about 14,000 years ago. If so, no human came near Southern Ontario before the gorges were established and the Laurentide Ice Sheet had receded north of Lake Huron. No evidence of human presence has been found in the Upper Grand region until about 11,000 B.C. The indications of these early arrivals consists of stone points left at sites occupied by caribou hunters. The mastodon and mammoth which roamed the land behind the retreating ice became extinct about that time. Perhaps they fell to the hunters' weapons—the first of the many extinctions in the New World due to human activity.

Beyond that, the First Peoples lived here for thousands of years without leaving much, if any, discernible imprint upon the landscape. Their legacy is largely confined to the sites of small settlements or temporary camps, often discovered only accidentally by a farmer's plough or a road-digging crew. From around 500 A.D. some groups adopted agriculture, and began to have a more enduring effect through the clearance of the woodland.

LAST DAYS OF THE FIRST PEOPLE

Europeans arrived this far west in the first half of the seventeenth century. At that time the Upper Grand lay on a well-used trade route which connected the Huron and Petun, or Tobacco, people to the north and Neutrals to the south. The gorges lay within Neutral Nation territory, known to early traders and missionaries by the Huron name Attiouandaronk, or "people who speak a different dialect." They had an agricultural economy and their main settlements were farther south, around the Niagara Peninsula. They probably used the gorges for hunting and, perhaps, they had places of religious significance here.

In 1626, a Recollet missionary, Father Joseph de la Roche Daillon, and his two French companions travelled along the Grand trail, the first recorded journey by Europeans. It is conceivable that enterprising French traders came this way a little earlier, but if so, they left no account.

From the route by which he arrived, or in his later wanderings, the famous Jesuit missionary Jean de Brébeuf may well have glimpsed the gorges. John Connon, in his book *Elora: The Early History of Elora and Vicinity*, even suggested that Brébeuf's mission began at a Neutral settlement where Elora now stands. I am unaware of any basis for this opinion. However, during their extraordinary efforts to preach and convert in the winter of 1640–41, Father Brébeuf and his young companion Pierre Chaumont travelled widely in this area.

The first permanent European settlers came to the Upper Grand in the early nineteenth century. They reported wigwams placed at Bon Accord and other locations along the ancient trail between Hamilton and Georgian Bay. Families and parties of First Peoples used this route, coming and going peacefully, usually pausing to trade venison and other game for vegetables. But, like the great forests that were consumed so quickly by axe, saw and lumber mills, their numbers became smaller and smaller. Finally their stopping places and the old trail were abandoned.

EUROPEANS IN THE LANDSCAPE

If the work of spoilation [sic] *and enclosure goes on a little longer unchecked, Elora's natural beauty will be worth less than nothing.*
The Elora *Lightning Express,* May 17, 1877

In the relatively short span of time since the end of the eighteenth century, humans have become the dominant geological agents over most of Southern Ontario. Perhaps the greatest change to the region's landscapes was the removal of most of the forests. Commercial logging came first; clearing of trees for farm settlement followed. By the 1870s, very little old growth survived in the Upper Grand. In many places along the gorges no trees remained up to their very edges. Photographs taken along Irvine Creek a century ago show

barely a single large tree left standing. A few scraggly remnants clung precariously to the cliffs and some clumps of trees grew along the floor of the gorge. There is much more greenery today.

As we have noted, this large-scale deforestation in the Grand basin, together with the near extinction of the beaver and agricultural settlement, brought substantial changes in the flow of the rivers. From the mid-nineteenth century, Elora, Fergus and neighbouring communities also experienced a wave of industrial growth. Water mills, quarries and lime kilns, coal gas works and factories spread along the rivers, and often tipped their wastes into the streams, bringing some severe air and water pollution. As early as the 1840s, the geologist Alex Murray had observed that "most of the beds of fossiliferous limestone...are well adapted for building and lime-burning, and are largely quarried for both purposes at Galt, Guelph, Elora and Fergus."

The economic prosperity and modernizing influences also brought people to Elora with an interest in natural history. As the 1877 newspaper quotation above indicates, some also began to cry out against the damage being done to their environment.

Earth Science at Elora

*At Elora, again, we are, I think,
considerably higher than at Guelph itself,
and since the higher we go among the
leaves of the rocky volume, the more likely
we are to find fossils of an advanced type,
it will be easy to see the peculiar
advantage enjoyed by an enthusiastic
geological student in our locality.*

David Boyle, *On the Local
Geology of Elora* (1874)

The Elora Gorge area played a small but fascinating role in the early study of geology in Canada. At first it was mainly thanks to officers of the young Provincial Geological Survey such as Alex Murray, who investigated the area in the 1840s and 1850s. After that, however, official interest lapsed. But a handful of local enthusiasts began, in the 1870s, to continue the work. A number of local residents, especially members of the Elora Mechanics Institute, took a lively

*David Boyle, LL.D. (Courtesy of Wellington County
Museum and Archives)*

interest in natural history and in the geological past revealed by the gorges. Two of them stand out in this regard: David Boyle, an artisan turned schoolmaster, and Thomas Connon, a merchant turned photographer.

Boyle, later to become Ontario's first Provincial Archaeologist, lived and worked in the area in the 1860s and 1870s. He investigated local prehistoric remains and the rocks and fossils in the gorges. The new educational theories of Johann Pestalozzi, who advocated direct observation of nature as the best way of encouraging students to learn, inspired Boyle's teaching in local schools. In time, his pupils at Elora Public School helped his contributions to geological science and the emerging field of archaeology. With nimble fingers and quick eyes they uncovered many hidden places and secrets of the gorge. Boyle donated fossils he and his pupils found to the Geological Survey. Many of the finds are now in the Royal Ontario Museum's collection. In 1875 the Museum of the Dominion Geological Survey in Montreal sent a generous collection of rock and fossil specimens, properly catalogued, for Boyle to display in the Elora School Museum. It was the first of its kind, though the survey went on to provide many other schools with such collections.

David Boyle's first publication, *On the Local Geology of Elora* (1874), seems the only predecessor to the book you are holding. It began as a talk delivered to the Elora Natural History Society, which he helped found in 1874. It was in this paper that Boyle expressed the view, still quoted locally, that the gorges were "... produced (for all I know, ten million years ago) by a sudden convulsion of nature—an earthquake." Boyle's observations on fossils, and how they showed the rocks had formed in a warm sea, were modern and seem close to today's thinking. Yet he still clung to old views that explained the main features of erosion and deposition upon the earth's surface as due to cataclysms, or to Noah's flood. The view that river erosion could, in time, carve such gorges, or that glaciers had moved across the land and changed its shape, were still in their infancy and even less widely accepted than Darwin's ideas.

The 1870s were, however, a time when great debates about evolution and the earth's geological history were receiving widespread and popular attention. Out of them came the daring ideas that shape our own notions of early life, as evidenced by fossils. More people were reading more books, especially the contentious ones by Charles Darwin or revolutionary geologists like Charles Lyell and Sir Roderick Murchison who had first recognized and named the Silurian.

At Elora, local naturalists discovered to their delight that the rocks and fossils they had found in the gorges and quarries related directly to the new theories and discussions in the great cities of Europe and the United States. But controversy surrounded their activities, perhaps more so in a small town. The struggle between the words of the Creation story in Genesis and Darwin's "heresy" formed the subject of many thundering sermons, and led to denunciations of these so-called free thinkers. Boyle and his friends had to tread very carefully.

Gerald Killan's biography *David Boyle: From Artisan to Archaeologist* drew my attention to these matters. I particularly recommend the chapter "Elora's Intellectual Awakening." Boyle was influential in starting a library in Elora, and while his museum seems to have been lost, the books later passed to the village. As recently as the 1980s the Elora Library still contained Boyle's legacy, including almost all of Darwin's books. When my family came to live in Elora in the 1970s, I was amazed to find such works in a small village library. But it was sad to see when the last persons had signed them out—in most cases not since the First World War!

For anyone interested in the landscape, the photographs by Thomas Connon and his son, John, are a priceless legacy. Thomas took a remarkable series of photographs from 1859 until his death in 1899. Many of the later ones illustrate the rocks

The Grand River between The Cove and High Lookout as photographed by John Connon in 1892. (Courtesy of Wellington County Museum and Archives)

and scenery of the gorges as Boyle and other late nineteenth-century naturalists saw them. Prints of the work of both the Connons can be seen along with other memorabilia in the Wellington County Museum and Archives. The University of Guelph's Archives house a large collection of the Connon glass-plate negatives.

But this begins to stray too far from natural history into human history, which is already well served. Hugh Templin's *Fergus: The Story of a Little Town* is not commonly obtainable. However, there is a 1975 reissue of *Elora: The Early History of Elora and Vicinity* by John Connon, Thomas's son and a close friend of David Boyle. It is edited and introduced by Professor Gerald Noonan. Mrs. Roberta Allan's *History of Elora* (1982) is available. Both cover a variety of themes in local history. Meanwhile, Elora is fortunate to have a resident professional historian, Steven Thorning. A member of the Village Council, his regular newspaper articles combine scholarly research with a wealth of personal knowledge and anecdotes. These articles, eagerly awaited, are high points in the cultural life of the village—signs, perhaps, that another "intellectual awakening" struggles to be born here?

EPILOGUE:
ENVIRONMENTAL CONCERNS AND
A HERITAGE RIVERSCAPE

*I can conceive of no more profitable and
pleasing way for a boy to spend a few hours,
than in such a place, where almost every few
minutes...exposes a gracefully formed shell.*
David Boyle, *On the Local Geology of Elora* (1874)

The appearance of the landscape in and
around Elora Gorge has undergone great
transformation in the twentieth century,
largely because of social changes. Not all
have been adverse. Indeed, it is likely that
the main gorges today look more as they
did in Brébeuf's time, 350 years ago, than at
any other time in the past 150 years. The
improvements are mostly a reflection of
economic conditions and land-use changes,
but partly of intermittent efforts at environ-
mental protection.

A period of economic decline in this
region, and centralization of the Ontario
economy after the First World War brought
the steady demise of many small industries.
As a result, their negative impacts upon the
local water, air and landscape diminished.
Unhappily, if the trees began to come back
and water quality to improve, settlements
like Elora went through a period of severe
economic hardship and depopulation from
the 1920s to the 1950s. When a resurgence
began in the 1960s, many empty, derelict or
dilapidated buildings dotted the landscape.

Elora is now a major tourist attraction.
Most of the main Grand Gorge lies within a
park managed by the Grand River Conservation Authority. A modest industrial
revival has taken place too, but with less
ugly consequences for the land, water and
vegetation than happened in the nineteenth century. Unfortunately, those of us
who have watched the gorge landscape
over the past couple of decades do see
cumulative and growing evidence of abus-
es. Especially by the end of each summer
there is more litter and broken bottles,
damaged trees, rubbish thrown down into
the gorges, and badly scarred and overused
trails. A steady pattern of encroachment by
construction, and artificial changes within
the gorges, blemish and compromise their
natural beauty. These threaten to get worse
if we do not encourage a better awareness
of our natural heritage, and engage residents and visitors in a desire to see it valued
and conserved.

A major problem, however, may be that
so many of us are now robbed of direct and
wholesome interaction with the landscape.
We have little occasion to develop the atti-
tudes and skills needed to appreciate what
is within immediate reach of our own sens-
es and thoughts. More and more of our surroundings are mediated by modern
technology and marketing. Our skills are
developed for working with and through
machines. In our schools, scheduling prob-
lems and curriculum requirements, as

The Grand Gorge in summer, looking downstream from The Cove before the highway bridge was built.

The Grand Gorge in winter.

much as the barrage of new tools and information or the sheer size of classes, deny most teachers the opportunity to do what David Boyle did so successfully in the nineteenth century. The rare field trip with a large class may cause as much frustration as learning. Many people seem not to know how to conduct themselves sensibly and safely or without harming the surroundings. They have not developed an eye for or interest in the wilderness scene, except to act out fantasies inspired by television and movies. They often seem disappointed that nature is not as neat as photographs can make it seem. They may pass by without seeing what is there, or do harm without realizing it.

With that in mind, I have tried to confine most of the material in this guide to things you can see, or to ideas that are based upon what is visible in the landscape. For we cannot really know our heritage, and whether it is being protected, without recovering the ability to relate to it directly.

Such remarks apply, of course, to a portable guidebook too! It will only serve its purpose if it tells just enough to inspire you to set it aside. Print is no substitute for sensitivity and enjoyment of exploring and trying to make sense of the unmediated natural scene. I hope the guide will be sufficient to help you get on with your own first-hand discovery of the ever-varying and always challenging Elora Gorge.

FURTHER READINGS AND SOURCES

The classic overview of the landscapes of Southern Ontario is:

Chapman, L.J., and D.F. Putnam (1984). *The Physiography of Southern Ontario*, 3rd ed. Ontario Geological Survey, Special Vol. No. 2 (and O.G.S. Map No. P.2715).

Additional materials on the bedrock geology and Silurian reefs are to be found in:

Shaw, E.W. (1937). "The Guelph and Eramosa Formations of the Ontario Peninsula," *Transactions, Royal Canadian Institute* 46, Vol. XXI 2, pp. 319–23.

"Silurian Reefs of the Great Lakes Region of North America," (1975). American Association of Geologists, Reprint, Series 14.

Sanford, B.V. (1976). The St. Lawrence Platform, in chapter VI, of Douglas, R.J.W. (ed.) (1976), *Geology and Economic Minerals of Canada*, Part A. Geological Survey of Canada, Department of Energy Mines and Resources, Ottawa, pp. 240-278.

The piecing together of the history of Ice Age events has been a major achievement of Canadian earth scientists. For our area, see especially:

Karrow, P.F. (1989). "Quaternary Geology of the Great Lakes Subregion," in Ch. 4 of Fulton, R.J. (ed.) (1989), *Quaternary Geology of Canada and Greenland*. Geological Survey of Canada, Geology of Canada No. 1, Ministry of Supply and Services, Ottawa, pp. 326–50.

Karrow, P.F. (1968). *Pleistocene Geology of the Guelph Area*. Ontario Department of Mines Geological Report No. 61.

Karrow, P.F., and B.G. Warner, (1988). "Ice, Lakes, Plants, 13,000 to 10,000 years B.P.: The Erie-Ontario Lobe in Ontario," in Laub, R.S. et al. (eds.), *Late Pleistocene and Early Holocene Paleo-ecology and Archaeology of the Eastern Great Lakes Region*. Bulletin 33 of the Buffalo Society of Natural Sciences, pp. 39–52.

On river work, there are two major references applying to the gorges:

Martini, I.P. (1977). "Gravelly Flood Deposits of Irvine Creek, Ontario," *Sedimentology* 24, pp. 603–22.

Greenhouse, J.P., and P.F. Karrow (1994). "Geological and Geophysical Studies of Buried Valleys and Their Fills near Elora and Rockwood, Ontario," *Canadian Journal of Earth Sciences* 31, pp. 1838–48.

Concerning rockwalls, the idea of active, inactive and relict cliffs is discussed in:

Emery, K.O., and G.G. Kuhn (1982). "Sea Cliffs: Their Processes, Profiles and Classification," *Geological Society of America Bulletin* 93, pp. 644–54.

Strength equilibrium slopes are treated in:

Selby, M.J. (1982). *Slope Materials and Processes*. Oxford University Press, Oxford.

For the early human history of our region see:

Harris, C. (ed.) and G.J. Matthews (cartographer) (1987). *Historical Atlas of Canada I: From the Beginning to 1800*. University of Toronto Press, Toronto.

ACKNOWLEDGMENTS

Writings on Elora Gorge itself are few, generally old, and not to blame for most interpretations here. Yet I have depended enormously on the work of earth scientists elsewhere in the region, especially syntheses concerning the bedrock geology by Dr. B.V. Sanford, and writings on the Quaternary history by Dr. P.F. Karrow, his colleagues and students at the University of Waterloo. Quotes from some early geologists come from an archival search by H. Julia Roberts, directed by Dr. Suzanne Zeller, a historian at Wilfrid Laurier University.

The Grand River Conservation Authority supplied the weather and river-flow data cited, and its personnel at Elora Gorge Park have been most helpful. Thanks to Wellington County Museum and Archives, and to archivist Bonnie Callen for assistance with early documents and to Douglas Scott for prints of early photographs.

I thank but cannot list all the Wilfrid Laurier University students and colleagues, local teachers and residents who have shared my interest in the gorges, but must single out Dr. Houston Saunderson, a fellow geomorphologist, whose good company and probing mind sustained my interest and improved my understanding of these and other landscapes for over two decades.

I thank Elizabeth Fasken, Peter Merry, Dr. Farida Hewitt and Nina Hewitt, for helpful comments on the text, and all of my family for their patience and encouragement.

Thanks to Carol Allemang for preparing the manuscript, to cartographers Pam Schaus and Rachel Moser for the maps and diagrams, and to the Department of Geography, Wilfrid Laurier University.

INDEX